Mine Eyes
Have
Seen the Glory

Mine Eyes
Have
Seen the Glory

ANITA BRYANT

Fleming H. Revell Company
Old Tappan, New Jersey

Scripture quotations in this volume are from the *King James Version of the Bible.*

To
the service of the Lord
and to my loving family
Bob, Bobby, Gloria Lynn, Barbara and Billy

Contents

Mine Eyes
Have
Seen the Glory

1

"Sing, Anita, Sing . . . ."

"THE BABY IS DEAD," the doctor told Grandma and Grandpa Berry. One look, and they could tell it was so.

I weighed nine pounds, but was black and swollen with poison. Stunned, my grandparents watched as the doctor laid me aside on a table, then turned and began to work frantically to save my mother's life.

At that point Grandpa, not yet a born-again Christian, sprang forward, shook his fist at the doctor, and called him a very bad name.

"If you don't bring my daughter and that baby around, I'll kill you," he threatened. The doctor shot Grandpa a brief glance, and continued to work over Mother.

"Get me a small pan of ice water then," he told Grandpa. "Mrs. Berry, make up the strongest coffee you know how. And bring me some whiskey."

Grandpa hastened to fetch the ice water. When the doctor dipped my head in it I caught my breath sharply. Immediately he slapped my bottom to make me cry. "Now get that coffee and whiskey down her somehow," he told my grandparents, "while I take care of your daughter."

Though it must have looked hopeless, Grandpa and Grandma Berry weren't the kind who quit. They kept pouring tiny amounts of liquid down me. Suddenly it all came up—coffee, whiskey, and the poison too. The doctor glanced around. "She might live," he said.

I'd made a dramatic entrance into an equally dramatic world—the raw, rugged Oklahoma oil country. My parents, Warren and Leonora Bryant, lived in Oklahoma City, where my father worked as an oil field roustabout.

They were such a handsome couple. Daddy, tall, outgoing in personality, always had an infectious smile and a manner that could win anybody to him. His friends called him Blackie because of his dark eyes and black, curly hair. By contrast, Mother had red-brown hair, light skin and green eyes, and a nature as quiet and introverted as Daddy's was exuberant.

In her quiet way, Mother almost worshiped Daddy. They had met in high school, courted there, and married right after they graduated. He was just nineteen and she eighteen when I was born, and they were still mighty young eighteen months later when my little sister, Sandra Jean, joined the family.

As the time for my birth drew close, Mother had gotten homesick. Daddy let her visit her parents in Barnsdall, Oklahoma, so that's why Anita Jane Bryant happened to be born in the big house where Grandma and Grandpa Berry raised Mother and her eight brothers and sisters.

It was a home where people really cared about one another, and after saving my life, Grandpa naturally seemed to dote on me. He even claims he started my singing career. My mother and her mother used to describe the scene.

"Sing, Anita, *sing*," Grandpa would croon, holding me tightly against his big chest and rocking me back and forth.

"Sing?" Grandma would tease. "What a thing to say to a six-month-old baby. John Berry, you're something!"

But Grandpa paid no attention to all that. "Sing, Anita," he'd urge, his voice very loving.

"Ah-h-h-h-ee-eee-ee . . . ," I'd suddenly respond, real loud, and Grandpa would shout with laughter. My first vocalizing seemed to tickle him half to death.

"Gracia, this baby was born singing," he'd announce triumphantly. "Listen to that. She's *really* got a big mouth on her!"

In the Berry family, a "big mouth" was quite a desirable attribute. Grandpa, an amateur song writer and song leader, headed up a large musical family, and there are also three preachers in our clan. I seem to remember that almost everybody either sang or played the piano, and several of the family occasionally sang on the radio. My mother's voice was as good as any; in fact, she and my sister had fully as much music in them as I had in me.

Daddy came from a big family too. The Bryants had seven children and, like the Berrys, knew how to enjoy life. Grandpa and Grandma Bryant had a well behind their house, and a bucket you let down for a long, cool drink of delicious water. A big watermelon patch adjoining their place belonged to the man next door; we kids would "steal" melons and eat them right there in the field, never dreaming that Grandpa's neighbor had told him to let us help ourselves.

I remember going to Wewoka to see my Aunt Violet and Uncle Vernon Wright and all the other aunts, uncles and cousins. Aunt Violet's house seemed to overflow with kinfolks, and had a lively atmosphere I loved. With our cousins, Sandra and I spent hours learning songs from the radio. The high spot of our week was listening to the "Grand Ole Opry" program out of Nashville, Tennessee, on Saturday nights.

Since we kids had nothing to entertain us except ourselves, when we weren't listening to the radio we usually played outside. We took turns riding an old wooden swing, made mud pies and "performed" the songs we heard on the radio.

I liked to sing the Grand Ole Opry numbers, especially the comical ones Little Jimmy Dickens presented. Using the back porch for my stage, I'd favor my cousins with such classics as "Sleepin' at the Foot of the Bed" and "Take an Old Cold 'Tater and Wait."

The first time I ever sang in public, however, was long before then, and thanks to Grandpa Berry. I was just two years old when Grandpa proudly prevailed on the preacher to allow his baby granddaughter to sing her first solo in the Baptist church there in Barnsdall.

Grandpa had encouraged me to sing "'Jesus Loves Me."

> Jesus loves me! this I know,
> For the Bible tells me so.
> Little ones to Him belong;
> They are weak but He is strong.

I was too young to be shy. If the congregation was surprised to see a two-year-old get up and sing, they must have been really startled at the big voice that came out of my tiny body!

Later on, Grandpa was proud of Sandra the same as me. For years she and I performed together in church and school. Though my sister is terrifically talented, there's always been a important difference between Sandra and me. She is shy and reserved like Mother, while I've always been a big ham.

From that first appearance at Grandpa and Grandma Berry's church, I knew I'd always sing wherever I could get anybody to listen.

I loved it. I always wanted to sing and never was bashful about favoring folks with a solo or two. Always, somewhere in the wings, I seemed to see Grandpa Berry, smiling, encouraging, bragging, saying, "Sing, Anita, sing!"

2

Family Ties

Soon after sandra was born, Mother and Daddy divorced. There had been real love between them, but I guess their young marriage had to endure simply too many strains. Daddy went into the army and Mother took Sandra and me to live with Grandpa and Grandma Berry.

There was more tragedy to come. Grandpa, who'd always made a good living with one of the major oil refineries, got caught in a terrible explosion which killed several men. He counted himself lucky to escape with his life, but his luck didn't hold far enough. Hot tar sluicing across his face destroyed Grandpa's vision.

Big, brash, family-loving Grandpa, the tough oilman who could outcuss anybody else on the job, was still pretty young when overnight he found himself totally helpless. The accident reduced him to almost total dependency; not only was there no way he could make a living, but he had to be led everywhere by Grandma or one of his children.

You'd have to know Grandma Berry to appreciate the faith and courage with which she met the situation. She was one of the last of her breed: a remarkable pioneer American woman. She gave birth to nine children, all at home, did her own housework, and managed proudly. Nobody ever once heard Grandma complain, nor saw her lose her temper.

Not only was she the world's best cook and a naturally accomplished wife and mother with love enough to spare for every member of her large household, but she was a genius at the art of living.

As Grandpa told Sandra and me many times as we grew up, it was Gracia Isola Berry's faith in God which joined in a mighty way with the tragedy that happened at the refinery that day, to produce a miracle in his life.

Soon after he went blind, Grandpa said, he experienced a Christian conversion. "I had to get my eyes put out before I could really see," he told us. And it was Grandma's faith—a huge faith that never wavered for an instant—that guided Grandpa Berry to God when he needed Him most.

Next to our own parents, Grandma and Grandpa Berry became the two greatest influences in Sandra's and my life. Daddy and Mother both were church-centered people who instilled a religious faith in us very early. But circumstances led us to Grandpa at a time when he was a babe in Christ—and what an enthusiastic, exciting new faith he had! Now the man who'd always been outspoken and frank, a tough oil driller who didn't hesitate to use bad language to express himself, became equally eager to tell how he'd been saved by finding Christ as his personal Saviour.

The family moved to Tishomingo, Oklahoma after Grandpa became blind. Some of the older boys helped out and Grandma taught Grandpa to grow a garden. Not only did he learn to grow crops he couldn't see, moving lightly and surely down long rows of corn, beans, tomatoes and everything else the good earth can produce, but soon he was able to lead Sandra and me through the woods to his favorite fishing holes where we'd catch fish for our dinner.

Sandra and I loved to get Grandpa to take us to town. We marveled at how well he seemed to see. Long before we could see a car coming Grandpa would have heard it, and he'd hold our hands firmly to stop us from crossing the street.

It's amazing how God provides for us long before we know what we're going to need. He did that for Grandpa. When Grandmother Berry was a little girl she didn't have much of an education, only as far as the fourth or fifth grade, and it was Grandpa Berry who really taught her to read and write. Later, when he couldn't read for himself, my grandmother used to do it for him. I can remember her sitting by his side in the evenings, reading his Bible aloud to him. Grandpa used to say she was his eyes.

So it was that my sister and I had a wonderful early life in small-town Oklahoma, surrounded by people who loved us, and knowing from the first that God loves us.

Even when we were tiny, people remarked on how different Sandra and I were in personality. Sandy is so much like Mother—talented, hard-working, sensitive, reserved. I, on the other hand, often seemed impossibly brash and was always ready to show off. "You were a born ham," Mother says.

There's absolutely no doubt that I was as aggressive a child as Sandy was retiring. Full of energy, always getting into mischief, stubborn, accident-prone, I'm afraid I made Mother a lot of trouble.

"You're too determined," she'd sigh. "Anita, you always go after what you want before you think what the outcome might be."

Headstrong, I would "help" Mother around the house, always insisting on doing things my way, seldom listening to instructions. Other times I would boss Sandra around, then claim we'd done the work together. Luckily, Mother had Grandma Berry's qualities of patience and loving kindness. She praised me for doing a good job whenever she honestly could, and refrained from harping on my bull-headed ways any more than she absolutely had to. Like Grandma Berry, she had the patience of Job.

The Anita Bryant temper got a good, early start, however. There was the time in the grocery store when I, age five, acted up so much that Mother actually took me behind the shelves and spanked me.

"You're *embarrassing* me!" I told her indignantly.

Another time that same year, my Uncle Hubert Berry got so tired of seeing my cousin Jimmy and me fight one another that he actually put boxing gloves on us.

"First one that cries gets a licking from me," he said. I blacked Jimmy's eye and that was that.

In a family big as ours, you knew you were loved—even if you did black Jimmy's eye, and even if you did boss your little sister around and sometimes lock her in the closet to scare her!

There was Grandma, always letting you experiment in the kitchen and cook all sorts of concoctions that you forced everybody else in the family to taste. There was Grandpa, who called you "the brave one," bragged on you, constantly had you sing at church. And always there were our mother and father, who loved us, reared us strictly, and treated both their daughters kindly and fairly.

3

Stage Struck

MY PARENTS REMARRIED the year I was three, and we all went to live in the town of Seminole, Oklahoma. Daddy worked there as a bookkeeper, and that's where we lived when I started to school.

That year the local high school needed a small girl to play a bit part in their operetta. They came to my school, and I tried out without saying a word to my parents.

I got the part and, ham that I was, felt thrilled. Probably thanks to Grandpa Berry, I'd always been willing to sing at the drop of a hat. Not only would I do church solos, I'd also offer to sing whenever Mother and Daddy had guests, or any other time I could buttonhole anybody.

Now I was going to get to perform on stage! I was supposed to be a gypsy's child, and Mother made me a costume. I sat on somebody's lap, sang one song, and spoke one line.

I remember that night very well. It didn't occur to me to get stage fright because I'd sung for so many people over the years. I loved my costume, adored wearing makeup, and was crazy about the audience. They applauded me. Young as I was, I liked it.

"I'm going to be a star someday," I told my parents after that performance.

From that moment on, I worked toward the goal. Nobody ever planted the idea in my head, nor did my parents ever push me towards a career in show business. They always helped me train my talents, always supported and encouraged me, but neither Daddy nor Mother ever pushed me.

From my second- through fifth-grade years our family lived in Velma-Alma, Oklahoma, in crude, cramped temporary housing near the oil field where Daddy worked. It was a little rough, living first in a two-room trailer with no bathroom facilities and then in a cramped three-room house, but that was the best we could do near the oil field. When we moved into the house and had a shower bath, I didn't know how to operate it. I scalded my back and ran screaming from the bathroom.

By contrast, Sandy and I remember well the beautiful farm that belonged to Mr. and Mrs. Joe Aldridge, a couple we met at the Church of Christ. Their children were grown and they had no girls, so Papa and Mama Aldridge took quite a shine to Sandy and me. They had us out for weekends. We learned to ride horses (my favorite was a palomino named Old Pet) and never dreamed, as we taught ourselves to ride bareback, that I was helping myself train for the rodeo jobs I'd do some day.

Although things were rough and there wasn't much money, Mother always produced costumes for Sandra and me when we needed them. We did a surprising amount of performing in those days. Sometimes it was solo, sometimes together.

Mother started keeping a scrapbook which over the years became crammed with clippings and souvenir programs; Sandy and me, featured at the 1949 high school senior class banquet, dressed in "grass" skirts our mother made and singing, "I Wanna Go Back to My Little Grass Shack in Kealakekua, Hawaii . . ." and, at the regular meeting of the Velma-Alma PTA, "Miss Anita Bryant sang 'Feuding, Fussin' and A-fightin.' "

As we appeared more and more often in school plays and civic programs, it got harder and harder to persuade Sandy to perform, and easier and easier to persuade me to.

"I'm going to be a star," I again told my parents.

It was about this time when the "star" learned one of her life's most important lessons. I was eight years old, and had persuaded Mother to take me to nearby Duncan, Oklahoma, to enter a radio talent show. It was a six or eight week contest, and I won each week. Dressed in the little Country and Western costume Mother made me, I'd sing "Bonaparte's Retreat" or some other such number, and each week I walked off with an exciting prize. I recall winning a record player, some records, groceries, cash . . . oh, the contests were fun!

By the time the final week arrived I'd gotten pretty cocky. I was learning a new song for the last show and I remember Mother asking me about it, the only time she ever did such a thing.

"Anita, are you *sure* you know that song?"

"Of course, Mother," I said, annoyed.

I shouldn't have been too certain. The show began, the band swung into my intro, and I moved toward the microphone. I started off with my usual eight-year-old self-confidence, enjoying myself hugely.

Then it happened. My mind simply went blank. I forgot my lyrics.

Even for an adult, that's a nightmare situation. Nevertheless, I didn't show outward panic. I simply turned to the band leader with all the poise I could muster and said, "Take it away, Leon!"

Then I bolted to the side of the stage, shaken to the

core. The band played sixteen or eighteen bars, the longest I ever heard, while I tried to recall the lyrics. Tears of shame and panic streamed down my cheeks.

At last I remembered the words, returned to the mike and finished my song. There was no great harm done, I suppose, except to my pride—which was devastated. It killed me to forget my lyrics, especially after what Mother had said. However, Mother didn't rub it in.

"Well, I guess you learned your lesson," she said with a gentle laugh, and that was all she said.

That lesson wasn't too far behind me when Lois Dix, the wife of one of Daddy's bosses, took Mother, Sandra and me to Oklahoma City so I could audition for the "Gizmo Goodkin Talent Show." It all seemed like an impossible dream. I had seen television before at my friends' houses, and now *I* might get a chance to appear on the screen. I got so keyed up by the idea that I promptly got carsick.

In Oklahoma City, I gave it all I had and was accepted on the show. I sang "Mississippi" ("By the M, I, crooked letter, crooked letter, I . . .") and people were nice enough to phone and write WKY-TV and say they liked me.

Now the world seemed to turn itself inside out for me. The station invited me to appear on other shows and Allen Clark, the music director, began to coach me with my songs. Mother and Daddy got excited about it. They talked it over and decided to move near Oklahoma City so Sandra and I could take dancing and singing lessons.

We moved to Midwest City, which is near Oklahoma City. It was exciting to look ahead to dancing lessons, to television assignments and other things I'd dreamed of doing, but it's not easy for a nine-year-old and a seven-year-old to move away from a town like Velma-Alma—a town we knew every inch of and loved. Sandra and I had lots of happy memories there.

One stands out for me beyond almost everything else that has happened in my life. It was at the Church of Christ in Velma-Alma that I was saved when I was eight years old.

When I told Mother of my strong convictions she questioned me closely. "Do you realize what a serious decision this is, Anita?" she asked me. "Do you really understand what you're saying? Do you really know Jesus?"

She asked me all the other questions any good mother would ask at a time like that, and I continued to assure her that I understood perfectly well what I was saying.

"Don't you want to wait until you're older before you take such an important step?" she insisted at last.

"Mother," I replied, "Can you show me in the Bible where it says how old I must be before I can be saved?"

Mother was stumped. All she could do, she felt, was consult our minister who answered, "That's good enough for me. I'll baptize her."

I well remember my baptism. I felt so clean inside, as though my sins were washed away. And as I walked down the aisle, conscious that I was making my commitment public—a matter of record—I felt the Spirit of God Himself leading me there. It was the most powerful feeling of my young life.

Now I am a mother, with children approaching the age I was that Sunday night I remember so well at the Church of Christ in Velma-Alma, Oklahoma. Because I remember that night, I know that even young children can know their Lord and serve Him, if their parents help them know Him.

I hope I handle this tender, high moment in my own children's lives with the same love and wisdom my mother offered me.

4

Oklahoma City

DADDY AND MOTHER were right about Oklahoma City. Sandra and I found one opportunity there after another to train our talents.

Right away we got involved in all sorts of things in school, performing at assemblies, plays, choirs as well as out in the community—everything from church services to civic club luncheons. When I was eleven I was selected as Red Feather Girl, and toured much of the state on behalf of the United Community Appeal. The next year I became one of two majorettes for The Kiltie Band, sponsored by American Legion Post Number 35, even as I became increasingly involved in television.

I loved every minute of our new life. Sandra and I took lessons at the Molly O'Day Dance School, and with some of the other kids there got to perform at Kiwanis luncheons and other such affairs all over the state.

Every week there were one or two exciting chances to sing, dance or otherwise perform. And at WKY-TV I started singing on a Country and Western show called "Sooner Shindig", and another called the "Scotty Harrell Show."

When Scotty Harrell moved on, they gave me his time

slot. I was twelve years old, had a fifteen-minute program each Friday night, and began to earn my own money.

It all felt great. I liked being able to buy some of the clothes and things we otherwise couldn't have afforded for Sandra and myself.

While it was fun to make money, however, I never thought of the money. What I really wanted most of all was a chance to sing, the thrill of performing, and—let's face it—the recognition.

Performers invariably seem to feel a great need for extra love and affection. In my own case, I feel an equal need to give it back. I want people to like me.

"God gave me a voice with which to sing," I reasoned, "and that's what I want to do." And as long as I kept my grades up and Mother could juggle my performance schedules and manage my costumes, my career zoomed along fine.

Yes, career. I was twelve, then thirteen, enjoying my own regular television program, earning my own money, and I certainly thought of myself as having a serious career.

The scrapbook got thicker. One newspaper feature written that year describes me as "small for her age . . . more interested in housework than in music." Another writeup describes a Future Farmers of America banquet in Sasakwa this way.

Pretty little Anita Bryant took the 700 packed-in guests under her spell, and they called her back with roars of applause until she finally threw them a kiss and left the stage.

I really don't remember any such heady occasion. What stands out most of all in my memory are my feelings of

26

intense ambition, and a relentless drive to succeed at doing well the thing I loved. I remember feeling very grateful to WKY-TV for opportunities to perform. Even then I realized how invaluable my television training might be.

Because my life already was directed toward adult-size goals, I sometimes had to miss out on some of the things thirteen-year-olds normally do. I was busy in junior high school, busy also with the choir, a local quartet and a number of assemblies and school plays, but sometimes it cost me a chance to knock around with my friends after school, or maybe to go swimming on Saturdays.

The image of myself as a star only seemed to grow brighter. I knew I had to practice and prepare myself.

Mother very wisely kept herself at arm's length about this. As always she was there, helping, supporting, allowing me to accept opportunities. But Mother never, *never* pushed me. I think she knew that pushing me would only make me hate the whole business—that it was no good unless it came from within myself.

So there matters stood. In some ways I was a rather mature little thirteen-year-old, rather well disciplined by my own choice. The year before, Sandra and I had joined the First Baptist Church in Midwest City, and I had committed my life to Jesus Christ. Everything in my life seemed to be on the right track, just as I'd have it be.

Then the blow fell. Sandra and I learned that our parents intended to divorce one another for the second time. Sandra and I felt as stunned and as desolate as Mother—and probably Daddy—must have felt.

In my self-assumed maturity, I cast about for possible reasons for this, and reluctantly I saw that our move to Oklahoma City might have been a large part of the cause. After all, Daddy took a half cut in salary so Sandy and I could have "advantages." Then too, once they arrived at Midwest City our parents never again found a church home. I saw there were some reasons for them to drift apart.

In our grief, Mother, Sandra and I came close together. Quite apart from the breakup of our family, the divorce hurt each of us in a special way. Mother lost the man she loved. Sandra, who always had idolized Daddy, lost the parent she was used to tagging around after.

Though I could only guess at their feelings, I can remember my own quite well. Was I somehow to blame for this? I asked myself. Did the breakup happen because of the excessive strains placed on our family by my own deep-felt hunger to perform?

These questions were too big for me to bear. For the first time in my young life I came to God in real anguish. I loved my father and felt he had rejected me, had rejected all of us.

Nevertheless, when the peace of God that passes all understanding came at last, I was able to understand my father somewhat and forgive him in love.

5

A Slap in the Face

LIFE GOES ON. Soon after the divorce, Daddy remarried. Mother worked as a statistical clerk at Tinker Air Force Base, and Sandra and I took over a big share of the housework.

It was a question of all having to pull together. Mother, Sandra and I always had been close to one another, and now we became even more so. If we hadn't, our ship might have sunk. With two teen-agers in the family, finances, emotions and energies easily could have been strained to the breaking point.

Mother, as usual, came through in fine style. Don't ask me how, but she not only worked full-time but also managed to be a real mother to both of us girls, always ready to consult with us, help us, and instruct us.

We'd reached those ornery early adolescent years, so she must have had her hands full. Sandy and I divided up the housework and took responsibility for ourselves, but that didn't mean we never bickered nor argued. We're two completely different personalities. Sandy is sweet and easygoing, while I'm more demanding and pretty much of a perfectionist.

Naturally, as most sisters do, we scrapped. At that age

Sandy might borrow my dress or sweater and leave it in a heap on the floor. I, on the other hand, often stayed up until midnight washing out underwear or pressing the clothes I wanted to wear to school the next day.

Despite our sisterly spats, we did stick together, though. We helped Mother do the housework, washed the dishes and our personal laundry, and cooked the meals. At the same time, Sandra and I were becoming increasingly active in school affairs, and my outside performances were beginning to require more and more time.

Somewhere in there, I remember, I perhaps began to get a little bit full of myself. "Little Miss Terrific," as I was billed in one promotion, appeared more and more often at weddings and civic luncheons and sang more and more frequently on live and televised shows. Pictures of a thin, somewhat gawky Anita with a big smile and very curly hair, showed up in newspaper ads. My name began to appear in news stories and features. All this, combined with my usual driving ambition plus that temporary little "stuck-up" period some teen-agers go through, momentarily turned my little head.

But Mother wasn't the type to let it stay turned.

I'll never forget the night she put me in my place. Mother had rushed home from work, hurried us through dinner, then raced me to the television studio for my regular show. Time was short, and as usual I was getting nervous and demanding. Both of us were tired, but Mother patiently helped me dress, then began to arrange my hair.

This was one of those nights. The more Mother worked on my hair, the less I liked the effect. The clock hands moved maddeningly fast towards show time, and Mother felt as conscious of that as she was of the critical scowl on my face.

"That hair looks terrible!" I snapped, when she finished.
Crack!

The slap sounded sharp as a bullet in the soundproof room. Amazed, I simply stared at Mother as tears welled up her eyes and in mine. She never had slapped my face before and she never had to do it again, but it worked. That slap told me I wasn't the Queen of Sheba, after all, and Mother was my mother—not my slave.

The moment the show was over we apologized very contritely to one another. "I know I had it coming to me," I told Mother.

"Anita, I'm sorry I hit you in the face," she said. "The good Lord provided a place for me to smack you when you need it. I'm sorry I slapped you like that!"

So our mother-daughter relationship was restored. Actually, I always could talk as freely to my mother as if she were a girl friend or a sister—but I always knew she was much more than that. She is my *mother*.

With a weaker, less levelheaded parent, I could have become quite spoiled during those years. Several individuals who really believed in my talent urged me to build and polish a repertoire for television and personal appearances. I worked hard at this.

In 1953 I cut my first record, a 45 rpm called "Somebody Cares." This simple little sacred song really did very well. This encouraged us to approach the major record companies, but they turned me down for a surprising reason. My voice was big and deep, and singing regularly in public all my life had given me a certain sophisticated sort of control. People would not believe this voice belonged to a thirteen-year-old, recording company officials said. They advised us to wait.

The next year, we went to Hollywood to storm the

movie company gates, and the verdict was very similar. I looked and sounded much older than my fourteen years.

I felt absolutely rejected. To add to my miseries, my adolescent appearance at times reduced me to utter despair. Not only had I become skinny and awkward, but my hands and feet were adult size. When the boys called me "Boats" —a name derived from those great feet—I smiled outwardly, but almost died inside. And, in common with many another teen-ager, I had ever present skin problems. I thought I looked terrible!

Worse, I had begun to notice boys in a big way . . . and they weren't asking me for dates. Sandra and I knew plenty of boys. Our house somehow became something of a neighborhood center for the kids on our block, so I had numerous boyfriends. They'd confide in me about other girls and ask my advice—which I freely gave. But still, they didn't ask me for dates.

"Mother, what's the matter with me, anyhow?" I asked one day. "They'll talk to me by the hour, but these boys won't ask me for a date."

"Stop giving them advice, Anita," Mother said. I followed *her* advice, and she was right. I had plenty of dates from then on.

Mother always understood my dreams and high hopes as well as my fears. She and Sandra backed me to the limit, often making real sacrifices so I could have what I needed in the way of costumes, clothes, time and emotional support. If I believed in my future, they believed in it too, and this was absolutely necessary to me.

All that made no difference at home, however. I had my performances; I had hours set aside for practicing; but I also had dishes to wash. Fair was fair, and Mother wasn't about to let one of her girls stick the other with an unfair share of the household chores.

I came to like housework, to enjoy cooking and cleaning, and it served a good purpose just then. The chores I had to do as part of our family life certainly helped me keep my feet on the ground.

This was a good thing, because the career tension built up rather steadily. Looking back, I marvel at how the Lord sent more opportunities every time I showed Him I could take on a little more responsibility. I didn't know that then, of course. I thought *I* was managing things rather well. Much as I depended on the Lord to help me through the tight places in my young life, I still didn't fully realize that my performing career belonged to Him, and that He was the author of all that was happening to me.

Yes, ambitious little Anita sort of thought she was managing things pretty well herself, through a combination of good luck and hard work. Then came the year I was fifteen, when something happened that I just knew would ruin it all.

Mother remarried. Sandra and I were so glad for her. Mother's self-confidence had suffered as a result of the divorce, especially when Daddy remarried within the year and acquired three new stepdaughters. Eventually Daddy and Jewel, his second wife, had a son, Warren, Jr., who is called Sonny. Though Sandy and I didn't grow up with Sonny, we're proud of our brother, who is smart, athletic and handsome like Daddy.

Now George Cate, "Daddy George," came into our lives, to make Mother happy again. He accepted us girls right off and let me know he was proud of my talent. We thought he was the greatest thing that could happen to our little family.

Trouble was, Daddy George's job would require us all to move to Tulsa.

"Mother, we *can't!*" Sandra and I wailed.

"We can't just move away from my television shows!" I argued.

"And all our friends!" Sandy wept.

Mother and Daddy George of course had to override our frenzied objections. We must do the thing that was best for the whole family, Mother pointed out. Besides, moving to Tulsa wouldn't be the end of the world. We'd see.

And we did. Soon after Sandy went to junior high and I enrolled in the Will Rogers High School, life began to take on exciting new dimensions.

We had cried our eyes out all the way from Oklahoma City to Tulsa. Now, to our astonishment, we discovered that things were going to be just great. For a starstruck kid like me, Tulsa, Oklahoma, was to be an absolute paradise.

6

Victory over Fear

IT'S FUNNY HOW the Lord seems to build your life like a mountain range, peak following peak.

I'm a real Sooner, an Oklahoman born and bred, and I love every inch of my state, from the rocky, bleak oil country to the lush greenness and urban excitement of the other areas I know. And few people realize that it's among the top five states in natural water resources. Oklahoma is many kinds of places, and I loved every one of them.

But it was in big, booming Tulsa, the year I was fifteen, that one "new girl in school" really came into her own. As a sophomore at Will Rogers High School, I felt like a kid turned loose in a candy store. Sandy and I soon became involved in various school activities. Our high school had terrific music and speech departments, so I majored in speech. That year I began learning to read music, and for the next three years I got to sing alto in the Allstate Choir.

Nor was it necessary for me to give up my television ambitions, as it turned out. In Tulsa I began appearing regularly on the "Chris Lane Show" over KOTV, and there were others as well.

With all this going for me, something else appeared on

the horizon. I thought it might be one of the most exciting possibilities of my life—or one of the biggest potential disappointments.

It was time to cast the senior class musical. At Will Rogers High, these productions always were enormously ambitious, and of near-professional caliber. This year the kids really outdid themselves; they bought amateur rights to *South Pacific*. The hit show was fresh from its long-running success on Broadway, and we would be the first amateur group to produce it. This really created a stir in Tulsa.

I felt excited, too, and determined to try out for one of the supporting roles. Now this took a little talking to myself, because despite all my prior experience, I suddenly felt shy. After all, I was new at Will Rogers High School, and I was just a sophomore. I knew full well there was no use to try out for one of the leading roles, which seniors invariably got. Still, I really wanted one of the lesser parts—if I could get it.

And that's where a little vanity crept in. After all, I considered myself a professional performer. *What if I tried out for a part and didn't get it?* It was even hard for me to admit to myself that I had these feelings. Also, it was hard to decide which might be worse, having everybody know I didn't get a part, or not getting one just because I wouldn't try. Of course, I didn't ponder this little dilemma too long before the ham in me won out, and I headed for tryouts.

As I climbed to the stage and threw myself into reading the role I felt I could best fill, butterflies landed full force in my stomach. I didn't even know the story of *South Pacific,* so in complete innocence I attempted the rather roistering role of Bloody Mary. "Bali Hai-i-i-i . . ." I sang, and hoped it sounded reasonably well.

Outside in the hall, I felt a light tap on my shoulder. Mr. Wyatt C. Freeman, who headed the school's music department, fell into step beside me. He had a look on his face which I couldn't quite interpret. (Now I know he must have been laughing to himself!)

"Anita, your voice is perfect for Bloody Mary," he said. "However, you . . . ah . . . somehow don't quite fit the part. Why don't you try out for Mary Martin's role?"

I felt absolutely flabbergasted.

"Those songs are too high for me, Mr. Freeman," I protested. "I could never make it. Besides, I'm just a sophomore. They've never had a sophomore play the lead. I really don't think I could do it."

In fact, I thought to myself, *I can't even imagine your suggesting such a thing.*

"I think you could," Mr. Freeman said quietly.

We sat right down on the stairs and began to discuss the demands of *South Pacific.* "Let me work with you on some of the songs," he suggested. "I have confidence in you. I think you can broaden your range enough to handle the lead. It will take hard work, but you can do it. Even if you don't sing too well during rehearsals, I believe you will do fine by show time."

I hardly knew what to say. I watched the dust specks dance down a strip of late sunlight that slanted in the window, and I considered Mr. Freeman's challenge. *You just think you've worked hard up to now,* I told myself. *Kiddo, if you were to get that part you'd have to work harder than you've ever worked before in your life. What's more, maybe you really can't do it.*

"Mr. Freeman, I just don't know," I stammered.

"There'd be so much to learn. It's a full-length script, acting and all, plus the songs. I'm just not sure my voice is up to that music, and even if I could do it musically, there's the expense. My parents might not be able to afford all those costumes."

"Just go on in and audition for the part, Anita," Mr. Freeman answered quietly. "If you get the role, we'll tackle the other problems one at a time. I feel sure you can do it."

So I tried out, and won the role. I just couldn't believe my luck. You see, beneath my self-confident young exterior lived an individual that very few people knew existed—a somewhat negative, scared kind of kid.

I had to hide all that, of course. The Anita Bryant most people saw was the brash, hammy, eager girl who so loved to sing, perform and reach out to audiences and make people enjoy themselves. I tried to keep everybody but Mother and me from knowing about the gloomy, pessimistic Anita who occasionally bugged the real me.

It doesn't pay to advertise your feelings of inadequacy. It's far better to battle and lick them—! So when such fears arose: *I'm too skinny . . . Why Can't I be really pretty? . . . I ought to do this song better . . .* I'd try to push them away. That's one reason I studied my songs until I knew them backwards and forwards, took scrupulous pains with my makeup and hairdo, and kept my clothes in such meticulous order.

But I had another habit far more important than these, which helped keep incipient feelings of doubt and inadequacy under control. Prayer became my chief weapon against fear. I began to pray more often, and certainly never went on stage or before the camera without first asking God for His blessing.

When my joy at winning the *South Pacific* lead died down and mild panic began to set in, I told myself God simply would have to help me once again. *He hasn't let me down yet,* I reflected.

He sent me real encouragement through Gordona Moore and Barbara Locher, two of my best friends who repeatedly told me they believed in me. My principal, Dr. Ray Knight, was a great help, too. And there was Miss Doris Niles, my speech teacher, who became a tremendous inspiration.

"Your real talent is for comedy," she declared. "Why, you have a flair for comedy you haven't even touched!" Miss Niles worked hard with me. She demanded my absolute best, told it like it was, and never gave false praise. In short, she was a real friend.

Never before in my life had I come so close to biting off more than I could chew. I threw myself into learning lines, songs, comedy routines, attending rehearsals, dance practice, more rehearsals, and all the while working, working, working with Mr. Freeman at the agonizing task of adding two or three full tones to the high part of my range.

I had to have those notes, because I couldn't sing the part without them. But could I get them?

The dismaying fact was that I'd sung for years without ever trying to expand or change my voice in any way. It was a fairly big voice, with plenty of range, and I just took it for granted. I simply reached in and pulled the notes out of me—that's all—and always they had been there, just as God gave them to me.

To deliberately attempt to do something new with my voice, oh, that was a frightening thought. But I *was* doing it. The hard work, the prayers I used when panic and discouragement prevailed, began to pay off.

Opening night arrived at last, and a talented senior boy named Don Pearson and I would share the spotlight. Before the show, my leading man and I peeped out from behind the wings. Don took one look at the packed auditorium and whispered, "Standing room only!"

Lord, you know what I've got to do tonight, I prayed silently. *Let me do my best. Help me always to live my Christian testimony, especially as I perform on the stage. Please give me courage.*

And, oh, yes, Lord, please help me remember my lyrics!

And then it was showtime: a blur of songs, dances, comedy, applause, lights, sweat, and the kind of joy I'd never before felt in my life.

For once I didn't mind being a skinny fifteen-year-old. Barefoot and dressed in a floppy sailor suit, my face very angular against the short, tightly frizzed permanent required so I could wash my hair on stage each night, I must have looked anything but glamorous.

But that seemed altogether beside the point. Each night for two weeks the packed houses, the laughter and applause, the songs and dances worked their same magic in my heart.

Take all the joy of singing at church with Grandma and Grandpa Berry, performing for the tribe of Bryant cousins, making Daddy's and Mother's company laugh. Then add in the contests, the television shows and all the personal appearances I'd ever had. Throw in the triumph of adding those important high notes to my voice range—just in time!

It all added up to almost more gratitude to God than one skinny fifteen-year-old could bear. Each night, from my heart, I know He heard me tell Him what I'd so often said to Mother.

Lord, I really do want to become a star.

7

My Toughest Decision

MY THRILLING ADVENTURE with *South Pacific* taught me an unforgettable lesson: when you rely on the Lord, He will not fail you.

But there's still another side to that, though it was a full year before I was to learn it: God also relies on *you* not to fail *Him*.

That was the last thought I had in mind, of course, the night I won a chance to fly to New York to appear on a big network television program, "Arthur Godfrey's Talent Scouts."

It seemed an unbelievable triumph, a great stroke of luck for a sixteen-year-old. My family was terribly proud of me, my friends all were excited, and I literally walked on clouds. Mother was to go with me as my talent scout, and I believe she looked forward to it almost as much as I did.

Then doubt crept in. At church, where our family was quite active, our pastor took me aside. He had misgivings about what I planned to do, he told me frankly. He wondered if I really should go to New York after all.

Up till now, he reminded me, I had not compromised my Christian testimony. Active in church work as well as school, civic, and local entertainment affairs, I had not experienced any conflict between what I stood for as a Christian and what I did as a performer.

But how did I know this always would be so? What if I went to New York, and show business success were to follow? My pastor wondered if I had given much thought to this. If I were to go to the top in show business, he asked me point-blank, did I think I could maintain my present testimony for Christ?

The question shook me. I sincerely respected this good Christian man, cared about his views, and knew he spoke to me out of love and real concern. By the time I left his study, I knew I could not evade the challenge he had made to my faith and character.

As the days wore on, several other well-meaning Christian friends made the same point with me. I began to feel gloomy, then distinctly irritated. And because I'm hardheaded, because I'm stubborn, at first I decided to pay absolutely no attention to them.

"I'm going to New York no matter what anybody says," I muttered to myself. "I deserve to go. I *want* to go. Why should I listen to them?"

Still, there was a ring of truth to what they told me, and despite myself, I couldn't quite shut it out of my mind. I refused to come out and admit it—even to myself —but the whole situation had me somewhat confused and frightened.

Certainly I didn't want to go against God's will for my life, as several people I respected seemed to think I was about to do. Certainly I didn't want to become any less of a Christian.

But that fierce drive in me—all that ambition—told me to go ahead. I had worked so hard for this oportunity. It made no sense not to take it. I *would* take it.

Then why was I so miserably unhappy?

Mother, perceptive as always, kept her own council until the day I finally blurted out to her the way things stood. Still she didn't lecture me, didn't offer me any opinion. I see now that Mother was wise enough to recognize that this must be my struggle and my decision. Knowing Mother, I'm positive she had prayed about how she should guide me in this.

"Have you prayed about this, Anita?" she asked in her quiet way. "Have you asked God to let His will be done in your life, instead of your own will?"

Reluctantly I confessed that I had done no such thing.

"I think you must," Mother said. "But Anita, don't just proceed to give God a lot of orders. You really must be willing to do *His* will. There's no sense asking Him what that might be until you know you're ready to obey it."

I could feel my heart sink right down to the floor. Mother was right, of course, but I just couldn't bring myself to pray about the problem. I wasn't ready to give up my wonderful New York trip, and I couldn't pretend I was.

That night I felt so unbearably burdened that I knew I could postpone things no longer. I went down on my knees beside my bed, feeling more rebellious and troubled than I'd ever felt before in my life. But heartbroken as I felt, I knew I couldn't carry that burden another step of the way.

Lord, please guide me, I prayed. *Forgive me for being so stubborn. I really do want to do Your will for me.*

Quite a few tears later, still on my knees beside my bed, I felt a tremendous, indescribable peace descend upon me. I knelt there, drained of all feelings and tension, simply waiting.

Suddenly I jumped to my feet. I felt absolutely washed

with relief and joy, because I knew just as well as I've ever known anything in my life that God fully intended me to travel with Mother and appear on the "Talent Scouts" program!

What God really wanted of me, I realized, was my submission. Of course he wanted me to have my professional opportunity, but also He wanted me to go, perform and act in full obedience to my inner guiding from Him.

That moment marked a turning point in my life. Fortunately, I first found God at a very early age, and I rededicated my life to Him again when I joined the Baptist church at age twelve. I knew He gave me a voice to sing with, and He helped my little career every step of the way.

Still, none of this would matter much, I realized, if I were to become unwilling to turn over my adult decisions to God. Now I understood my burden. I had feared the consequences of going against His will. God is just. He will be obeyed.

Then it was that I felt overwhelming gratitude that I had surrendered myself once more to Him. Obviously it would have done me no good to go to New York in that tumultuous state of mind. I knew I had been saved, but saw that the devil might have used anything—my ego, ambition, any of the natural desires a young girl has —to turn me away from Christ.

That's what my friends feared, of course, and I know now that they were quite right. It *is* difficult to maintain your Christian testimony in show business. The devil has attempted to beguile me, through this work I so enjoy, more times than I care to remember.

But what my friends didn't realize, and what I was too young to know, is that through Christ you can do anything and that even the most unlikely situation can become a vehicle for His work.

Sometimes now, when I face making a really tough decision, I think back to that night in my bedroom. Then I made a crucial decision—one I could not have postponed. Such basic steps must be taken early in a Christian's life; they lay the groundwork for the important decisions that will be made later.

I don't always like deciding things, of course. Being stubborn and impetuous, I'm apt to go off on tangents in my life and work myself into predicaments that seem impossible.

Lord, what do I do now? I ask. *You see I just can't cope with this!*

I've learned that when you do absolutely everything you know to do, you'd better ask Christ to take over and help you out of the muddle. Lots of times I simply flounder until I remember to rely on Christ. It's so human to be guided by our likes and dislikes instead of asking for His perfect direction.

God in His wisdom wanted me to go to New York, and today I believe I know why. He wanted me to be aware that I could aim for success in show business and still face, through Christ, all the challenges and temptations there are.

He wanted me to turn everything over to Him, and to say, "I can do all things through Christ, which strengtheneth me." That New Testament verse (Philippians 4:13) has become my very favorite. I rely on it, and it is true.

When I told Mother what had happened in my heart, she rejoiced and was satisfied. Little did either of us dream what God foresaw for me as a result of that trip.

Going out in submission to His will, I watched as He

opened doors for me that I never dared hope would open. For example, after my "Arthur Godfrey Talent Scouts" appearance, I got to visit his popular morning show every day for a week before I had to return to Tulsa and to school.

That began a series of periodic appearances on the Arthur Godfrey CBS morning programs whenever I could get away from school. As long as I kept my grades up, I was able to get this invaluable experience pretty frequently during my junior and senior years in high school.

Also, before I graduated I got to appear as a guest on the "Don McNeill Breakfast Club" show. These two big network shows, both enormously well liked across the country, launched me nationally in a wonderful way.

During my senior year in high school I signed on with MCA, the big artists' agency, and got my first recording contract with Carlton Records. And all this time I stayed quite active in school affairs.

Not many teen-agers could possibly feel much luckier, happier, or busier than I did. I marveled then, as I still do today, that God would open such perfect doors for me in show business.

8

I Decided to Bluff

AN INTERESTING THING about show business is the fact that anything can happen, and frequently does. Good, bad, boring, funny—you name it, and it probably has happened to me.

So I lived with a great sense of expectation—yet never could I have anticipated what happened to me next.

The fact is, I entered the Miss Tulsa Pageant. I'd never entered a beauty contest before, nor did I ever expect to. But I had graduated from high school by now, life seemed comparatively calm, and some good friends at Radio Station KAKC urged me to involve myself in this.

I soon had second thoughts, of course. I'd always been on the skinny side, and I had no illusions about my looks. I knew what was good, what was bad, and what might get by. Gradually, once again, the negative side of me began to rear its ugly head.

Although I disliked the thought of not winning, it was not realistic to expect that I could. But since my folks had always given me so much, and since they couldn't afford to send me to college, I felt I should try through the pageant to win a scholarship. It would be nice to go away to school, I thought, to major in music and speech, and to prepare for my career.

Station KAKC sponsored me, so I resolved to try hard for them. Then I'd think about parading down the runway in a bathing suit, and my courage would start to drain away. Oh, I didn't object to wearing a bathing suit. What's the difference in appearing that way before the judges and being seen at the beach? It was just . . . well, I felt all too painfully aware of each flaw in my face and figure. Suddenly they mattered terribly.

Sound trivial? Well, to a performer, everything matters. It has to. You get a sort of stark objectivity about your looks, your act, your abilities and weaknesses, because you must maintain a healthy self-criticism in order to keep improving.

Every woman likes to be told she's beautiful, and I'm certainly no different from all the rest. But I truly hope that people can see some inner beauty in me—the kind that comes from love and character. That sort of beauty lasts, whereas mere glamour never does.

As I prepared myself for the Miss Tulsa pageant, enthusiasm took over and my first misgivings began to fade. You have to admire anything that is done on such a high plane, and I could see the pageant would be great experience, a means of meeting some fine girls, and just plain fun.

It became all that and more. My sponsor provided part of the extensive new wardrobe I needed. There were fittings, rehearsals, photographs and interviews. Everything possible had been done to prepare each contestant, I told myself the night the pageant finally arrived. No wonder everybody looked so deceptively calm and smiling—and so beautiful!

Like most other things I've ever felt apprehensive about, the affair was nothing at all to dread. In fact, I really hadn't anticipated it very accurately at all—especially the climax.

I was relaxed by that time, feeling absolutely happy for myself and all the other girls. There was a drum roll . . . a pause . . . and then. . . .

"Ladies and gentlemen, may I present Miss Tulsa!" the emcee announced. "Miss Anita Bryant!"

Somehow lights got bright, flashbulbs popped, and applause swelled with the music. I was smiling, and smiling, dazed and altogether unbelieving, and then Mother's arms were around me, and Sandra and Daddy George just beamed.

The thing that couldn't happen *had* happened to me. Now it seemed I'd have to enter the Miss Oklahoma pageant. This time the Tulsa Jaycees sponsored me and got Toni Spencer, a former Miss South Carolina, to teach me the ropes. I felt I owed it to everybody to redouble my efforts, and Toni helped me do just that.

At a time like that, every friend you have rallies around. They wish you luck, offer to lend you their best clothes, slip a folded bill into your hand to help with expenses, or hug your neck and tell you they're proud of you.

It humbles you. You know you don't deserve all that unselfish love, and you don't forget it for a moment. It stayed with me clear through all the procedures, and through the instant when—incredibly—they crowned Anita Bryant Miss Oklahoma!

Many, many girls dream of entering the Miss America contest at Atlantic City, New Jersey, but never had it been part of my dreams. The idea simply never entered my head. Now, through some amazing fluke, it seemed I was going. The First Christian Church of Oklahoma City would sponsor me and Dolly Hoskins, who ran the Miss Oklahoma Pageant, would be my chaperone. I decided to bluff my way just as far as I could possibly go—and beyond that, to have a ball.

But first came the hard work of preparing myself—and it was some of the hardest work I ever did. Toni Spencer told it to me straight:

"You're going to need a lot more this time than just your good looks, talent and winning personality," she said. "I expect you'll do okay in those categories.

"But Anita, the judges also will be interested in your mind," she told me frankly. "They'll expect you to know something about world affairs, and to have some opinions. You've kept yourself too confined to the state of Oklahoma. You're simply not aware of what's happening in the rest of the world."

It was absolutely true, and I knew it. At age eighteen my approach to life seemed hopelessly naive and provincial compared to that of most of the other contestants. Almost all of the other girls had had some college education, and many of them held degrees. Since I was one of the youngest girls in the pageant that year, relatively unschooled and unprepared for high-level competition. I considered myself lucky to have a chance to watch the others in action. I wanted to pick up all the pointers on poise and finesse that I could, because it would be useful in my future career.

After exhaustive grooming, coaching and preparation, at last the girls from the then forty-eight states of America proudly went through their paces. As event succeeded event, as beautiful girl after beautiful girl bowed out of competition, the field narrowed to ten finalists.

To my dazed delight, I'd made it to the top ten. What spectacular, unexpected luck! The Miss America finalists got to televise their talent entries to a fantastically large, nationwide audience. I never before had performed before so many Americans. I felt boundless gratitude for this development.

From that point on, events moved like a dream. Again the smiles . . . cheers . . . music . . . applause . . . and Mary Anne Mobley wore the Miss America crown. But crazily, incredibly, somehow *I* got to be second runner up!

I simply couldn't comprehend it. Days before, I'd traveled to Atlantic City determined to work hard and simply enjoy myself. As I met one gorgeous girl after another, all seemingly formidably smart, poised and well dressed, it was obvious to me that these girls really were Big League. Not only did they possess beauty and brains, but most had the sort of character and personality that represents the very highest type of American.

I could only wonder, therefore, at what had happened to me. When some of my friends, loyal to the end, expressed disappointment that I'd come so close to winning—only to "lose" so narrowly—I just could not agree.

For one thing, no Miss America Pageant entrant could possibly lose. The whole thing represents a rare experience and privilege for any girl lucky enough to get there.

Through the pageant, I met some wonderful new friends I enjoy to this day. I learned a lot, through competing against some of the finest human beings I ever met, in a spirit of mutual admiration. It meant a great deal to me that I tied for the title of "Miss Congeniality." And very obviously, the television appearance could really mean a potential boost to my career.

No, I never felt I "lost" the Miss America contest. Indeed, I never asked God to let me win. However, by "losing," as it turned out, I "won." God had a wonderful new door for me to enter. Had I reigned as Miss America, that door could not have opened.

9

Till There Was You

THANKS TO THE Miss America Pageant, I got the college scholarship I'd hoped for. Soon I enrolled at Northwestern University in Chicago, where I planned to major in speech.

But even before that, another terrific opportunity had arrived—a regular spot on ABC's "Don McNeill Breakfast Club" show, which originated in Chicago.

Such a double stroke of good luck put me on cloud nine, except for having to leave home. The little poem Mother wrote about that seemed to put things nicely into perspective.

ANITA

When things are packed and you are ready to leave,
Don't look back, but look forward to the things you can
  achieve.
Your family loves you and wants to help all they can,
But you yourself will have to do it with your own hands.
For then you will feel that you have climbed the ladder
And it wasn't handed to you on a silver platter.

My thoughts, my love and my prayers go with you each day
As you climb your ladder along the way.

Be sweet and kind to everyone you meet,
But be alert, for there are those who want to see defeat.

If time of trouble should appear,
You know your family is always near.
My ears and arms will be open, have no fear,
For I am and will always be your MOTHER, dear.

Life had begun to get rather marvelously hectic, I thought. Though I'm not exactly the best first thing in the morning, you sure didn't hear me complain. Nope, I was too busy thanking God for such a good break—one that didn't interfere with my school schedule, at that.

Northwestern, a large university with a very beautiful campus and an excellent curriculum, seemed just right for me. It disappointed me a little that, because of my radio commitment, it seemed best to live near the studio instead of in the dorm. I rented a one-room efficiency unit off campus and tried not to mind. When one of the sororities gave me a bid, that sort of made up for things: I really wanted to enter into campus life—to get to know some of the students.

Then I attended my first fraternity party, and that changed everything. There was lots of beer drinking, girls sat on men's laps, and everybody's behavior, I thought, seemed much too free. They were just doing their thing, I guess, but it offended my small-town sense of propriety.

I felt so miserably out of place at that party that I decided simply not to get involved at all in the social whirl. I didn't pledge the sorority. Maybe I was too serious-minded—I don't know.

Nowadays I have to smile to think back on the irony of the situation. Here I was, involved in show business, living off campus—yet going to church every Sunday. And I didn't take to sorority life, because it seemed too fast!

So I was lonely. It was a difficult time for me. Don McNeill and his wife Kay sensed all this. They befriended me, as did several of the show's musicians and their families, and they'd invite me to spend weekends at their homes. All these people came to be like relatives to me.

What makes people nice enough to feel concern for a lonely kid? I think of Kent and Dolly Tomlinson, for example; when I mismanaged my funds and ran out of money, Kent would come to my rescue and offer a loan.

Then there was Tommy Thomas, the drummer, and his wife Mary. Tommy became saved after I joined Don McNeill's program, and he said I had been a tremendous influence on him. My good friends, the Roy Baumanns, led Tommy to the Lord.

I had to get up at 4:30 in order to get to the show by seven each morning. Afterwards we'd run over our music for the next day's program, and then I'd scoot to my eleven o'clock class. Because I had to be in bed every night by nine, there was little time for dates, parties or fun. Consequently, the McNeills and the other great people on the Breakfast Club meant more to me than I ever could say.

They kept me on my toes, because I had a great desire to match their professionalism on the air. Yet they knew the great art of relaxing and enjoying their work to the hilt.

One morning, for example, I overslept. To my horror, the phone rang and I heard the cheerful voice of Cliff Peterson, the show's producer.

"Rise and shine, Anita. It's seven o'clock!"

It was like a nightmare. Feverishly I threw on my clothes, jumped into my car, and broke all sorts of driving records in order to get to the studio before air time. I was too late for rehearsal—hadn't even stopped to put on my makeup —and we were on the air.

Well, the whole crew proceeded to kid me unmercifully during the show. My tardiness became such an hilarious joke that I almost had forgotten the humiliation of it and begun to enjoy myself. Then my pixie host sprang one last prank. With great glee, he produced the ugliest, loudest alarm clock you ever saw, and presented it to me on the air. We all broke up. Needless to say, I never was late again!

As that year wore on, an astounding thing happened. The record I had cut for Carlton Records moved up to the million mark in sales.

Now Joe Carlton had done a very smart thing. He knew I was a straight singer who didn't like to do rock and roll, and he never tried to persuade me to change my style to conform to popular tastes. Instead, he let me sing a ballad, the kind I loved, just as I wanted to sing it. We chose "Till There Was You" from *The Music Man.*

Amazingly enough, this song already had been recorded thirty-three times, but never before with a backbeat so it would appeal to teen-agers as well as to adults. When it hit, it hit big.

Once again, I could see the Lord's hand guiding my life. Had I won the Miss America Pageant, according to terms of the contract I could not have performed (certainly could not have recorded) for a year. During that time, Miss America's appearances and performances are under the strict sponsorship of the pageant, and her talent belongs to them exclusively.

You can see it might have been very bad for my career for me to win the Miss America crown. The best possible thing for me was what happened instead—the experience gained at the pageant, exposure on national television, a college scholarship, plus a clear track so I could cut more records and make more TV and personal appearances to back up my first hit.

Once your success begins, you really have to get down to work, I discovered. Weekends I began to go out and do the record hops, such as the "Dick Clark Bandstand" to plug the record. On top of my already stringent schedule, this nearly ran me ragged. That's why I left school before the year was out. There were simply not enough hours in the day, so often something had to suffer—either singing or my college work.

I'm reluctant to admit that I gave up college, and I definitely do not suggest that other young people should follow my example. Still, I felt led to pursue my career with all my energies, and that's what I did.

The record hop circuit is strenuous, but I did it because I knew the importance of grabbing the attention of the major disc jockeys who choose the songs which are played on the air.

One of the first of these fellows to plug "Till There Was You" was a certain disc jockey named Bob Green of Station WINZ in Miami, Florida. I knew Bob Green by reputation—knew he ranked as one of the country's top ten deejays, and that he had a terrific radio following. I felt really elated to learn he was giving my record a big play. Little did I then realize just how he eventually would come to figure in my life and career.

Meanwhile, I'd squeeze in a few dates whenever I could —maybe a soda date on campus at five in the afternoon, or a weekend movie with Tom McNeill, who is Don and Kay's son. In fact, by that time I was going pretty steadily with Nick Todd, who is Pat Boone's brother. We had met at church and were getting rather serious about one another.

At that point I flew home to Tulsa to help crown the new Miss Tulsa. Bobby Darin, there to take part in the ceremonies, asked me for a date.

"That's very nice of you, but I'm flying to Miami right after the pageant," I told him. "I'm appearing for Carlton Records at the big disc jockeys' convention there."

Now there never has been anything else like that convention, before or since. Every top star and recording artist in the world had arrived to represent the top labels. The show was to start early in the evening and go until six in the morning. It would open with the Kirby Stone Four, and I would be second on the bill. I was the only unknown artist on the whole program.

Connie Francis, Pat Boone, Errol Garner, Peggy Lee, Frank Sinatra—everybody was there. And because I was the top recording artist for Carlton Records, a small company, and because my record had hit the million mark, I got to mingle with all those stars. You can imagine how I felt.

At the Miami airport, Joe Carlton and Juggy Gales met my flight. He had Bob Green, the important disc jockey, in tow, because he felt it would be good for my career if Bob got to know me personally. I don't know what Bob thought about me, but I took one look at him and thought, "Oh, wow! He's much too good-looking to be a nice boy."

Because Bob Green was just about the best-looking man I'd ever met, I was leery of him from the beginning. Blond, tanned and slim, with a personality just as great as his looks, he seemed almost too attractive. I liked the sharp way he dressed, his casual but authoritative manner, even the sporty white convertible he drove, with his name lettered on the side.

As we rode toward my hotel, Bob asked me for a date that evening. Although I wanted to accept, I was afraid.

"I have to do a show this evening, and don't even know all the details yet," I told him evasively. "I can't say for sure." After all, I didn't want to brush him off completely.

"You have some time before rehearsal," Bob suggested. "Why don't you let me take you to the beach?" Since that seemed both reasonable and safe enough, I agreed.

When I met my handsome escort in the hotel lobby a little later, it was only to see him besieged by a crowd of screaming, autograph-seeking girls. That definitely made an impression on me. I could tell he was used to this sort of thing, and I thought he handled it very well. Obviously Bob Green must be terribly popular, I thought.

At the beach, we immediately ran into Pat and Shirley Boone. I didn't want them to think I was fickle, so I made a great point of introducing Bob as "one of the country's top disc jockeys." So from that point on, I acted standoffish and cool toward Bob, who became more and more puzzled by my attitude. When he wanted to take my hand and run into the water, I declined. When we did go into the water at last, the red color rinse on my hair started streaming down my face. What an impression I must have made on Bob! He must have thought I was a real hick.

To my surprise, he asked me again about a date that night. Because I was nervous about the show and unsure about Bob, I decided to do the prudent thing. I gave him a very polite brush-off.

My part in the glamorous show came and went very early that evening. Dressed in a long ball gown, I clutched the microphone nervously and regaled some of the world's best singers with songs from my one hit record—first, "Little George Has the Hiccups" which was the flip side, and then "Till There Was You."

Then, for me, it was over. I sat with the Carlton Records officials at their reserved table, watching the ballroom change as people drank a little more, talked a little louder, and filled the air with cigarette smoke. I began to feel tired, hungry, and a little bored. Then Bob Green walked by, not looking toward our table.

I came to life. "There's Bob Green, the disc jockey," I told one of my companions. "Why don't you invite him to come to the table?" He reached Bob just before he got to the door. Nonchalant and cool, rather indifferent to me— nevertheless, Bob Green joined us.

So I made a little effort to be nice. In fact, we relaxed and had a great conversation. Then, all at once, I realized an interesting thing—that Bob Green neither smoked nor drank.

Now that's certainly no criteria for decency, nor is it the only character reference—but I considered it most unusual. That seemed somehow out of character for a top deejay who was known to be a swinger with the girls. This Bob Green was beginning to interest me.

It didn't take Bob, smoothie that he was, long to get me out of there. When he suggested that we go find something to eat, I jumped at the idea. Soon, seated in his little car, we headed into the most beautiful, soft, romantic night you ever saw, complete with an enormous full moon and the sound of waves hitting the beach. The setting was picture perfect—and I fell asleep in the car!

So far as Mr. Green was concerned, that really must have put the cork in the bottle. When the sound of the car radio woke me, I could see that Bob was distinctly annoyed. Still, he was very nice about it.

At the hamburger place, more people came over to ask for Bob's autograph. When he very graciously introduced me, they said, "Oh yeah, you're the gal who sings the song about the bells on the hill."

So I felt a little better. I liked having strangers recognize me in front of this celebrity I was with. Maybe the evening wasn't a complete dud, after all.

We walked along the beach near my motel. We walked, and talked, sat down on a bench, talked some more, and suddenly the hour was terribly late. It was hard to believe this sophisticated deejay could turn out to be such an interesting guy—and so nice. I really hated to say goodnight. When he offered to drive me to the airport the next morning, I accepted with real pleasure.

"If you ever come to Chicago, please let me show you around. You've been so very nice to me," I told Bob just before I boarded my plane. Quickly I scribbled my name and address for him, though I really never expected to hear from him again.

When the phone rang in my apartment the next evening, I was startled to hear Bob Green's deep voice on the line.

"Why in the world are you calling me?" I asked in some surprise.

"Oh, I just wanted to talk to you." Our conversation between Chicago and Miami must have lasted an hour. The next evening, and the next several, he phoned again. Soon I began to think Bob had taken it upon himself to support the entire telephone company. Also, he had begun to write letters to me.

Much as I liked it, I knew it was time to stop leading this nice guy on. Though I hated to, I told him I was sort of unofficially engaged.

"That's all right. You're really in love with me," he said, with a little laugh. So we joked the situation off, and I continued to accept his letters and phone calls.

At last the situation began to seem somewhat ridiculous. When Bob took his vacation and flew to Chicago, I stuck to my offer to show him around. He took me to dinner and the theater. I invited him to the Breakfast Club, and we had a lot of fun.

However, I knew it was time to get firm. I let Bob know I really was quite serious about Nick. Further, I had to fly to New York that weekend for a personal appearance, and Nick and I had a date. It definitely was time for Bob and me to cut our friendship off, I felt, before it got out of hand.

The idea didn't seem to perturb him too much.

"I need to go to New York myself. I'll just fly along with you," Bob told me. So he sat next to me on the flight and wrote little love notes to me the whole time. I began to burn. I tried to ignore him.

Just before the plane touched down, I turned to Bob.

"I'm sorry, but all this has got to stop," I told him, and I meant it. "I never want to see you again. I'm really sorry, but this is the way it has to be."

My words didn't seem to ruffle him a bit. He just told me where I could reach him that weekend in Atlantic City, if I needed him. *Doesn't the man even listen to me?* I wondered. *I'll never phone him!*

When Nick and I saw one another that weekend, we both somehow realized that what we felt was not love, but a real friendship and respect augmented by a certain amount of infatuation. It was a mutual realization, and not at all painful.

Later, feeling quite foolish, I placed a phone call to Bob

Green in Atlantic City, where he was staying with Fabian and his manager, Bob Marcucci.

"Why are you calling me? I thought you told me to get lost," he said somewhat sternly.

"Oh Bob, I just missed you. I thought I'd call to see how you are." Even as I said it, I realized how lame that sounded.

There was a pause. We both laughed. It felt pretty good to be back in the good graces of one of America's top deejays!

10

Love and Marriage

I DIDN'T FEEL ready for a serious courtship. At nineteen, with a steadily climbing career and a full course of college classes, life had gotten so hectic that it was all I could do to find time to date occasionally.

Besides, this Bob Green character lived and worked in Miami, while I lived and worked a couple of thousand miles away in Chicago. Not only did we actually have no time for this foolishness, most of the time we stayed halfway across the United States from one another.

So what did we do? Courted by telephone and letter, that's what. The time we actually spent with one another that first year totaled less than three weeks, including Bob's vacation!

Then, the following fall, I took off from the Breakfast Club and went home to Tulsa to have my tonsils removed. Bob showed up there—and I didn't even invite him! He simply decided he was going to marry me, and this seemed like a good time to meet my parents.

Though I loved Bob, the idea of marriage was something else again. I guess I fought the idea because deep in the back of my head I had strong reservations—not about him—but about marriage.

I really wanted to wait until I was about twenty-five. I wanted a lasting marriage. At that point in my life, I couldn't believe my career ambitions and all the rest of it could combine very well with being a wife and mother. In short, I was young and scared.

I'd never thought about marrying somebody in show business. *A profession entirely removed from my own would be better,* I thought. Since that wasn't a terribly realistic idea, it illustrates that I'm something of a dreamer. Bob Green, however, is realistic.

He is also enormously energetic and aggressive. Despite the problem of the miles between us, Bob cared enough to spend the time, energy and money to pursue me.

That frightened me too. I could see I cared for him enormously—was really beginning to fall in love very deeply—and I just didn't want to. I fought him like crazy, every step of the way.

So when Bob came to Tulsa, I felt a little mad about it, really, though I also wanted him to meet my parents. Yet I knew if he didn't push me, our relationship probably never would go any further—because I really didn't want to get married.

So Bob came to Tulsa. Tired, troubled, and sick as a dog, I felt about as romantic as an old dishrag. The visit lasted through part of the Christmas holidays. One day he showed up with a big, gorgeous package, which proved to contain a mink stole.

Now Bob never lets any grass grow under his feet. If you think I felt confused and overwhelmed that he'd bought me this expensive fur, imagine how I felt when I noticed he'd had my initials embroidered in the lining— A.B.G.! I could have killed him—I was so embarrassed.

You see, Mother didn't know anything about us—how

serious we were or anything. She tried to laugh off the stole incident, but I could see she didn't like it.

Every now and again I'd catch Mother giving one of us a speculative look, trying to figure this thing out. I could guess what she thought: that Bob Green came on a little strong; that he was too much the glamour boy. While he appeared to be nice enough. Mother decided he must be a little fast. This wasn't the kind of man for *her* girl—a man who'd rush out and buy a fur stole, for goodness sake!

As I looked at Bob through Mother's eyes, it was easy for me to see how suave and aggressive he seemed to her.

"You'd have to know him, Mother," I told her. "He's really just the opposite of what he seems to be. A big-time deejay has to look and act kind of sharp, but beneath it all Bob's just a small-town boy."

This was true, I realized. Bob, like me, was thoroughly caught up in show business. He enjoyed his success, but deep down underneath, he really wanted simpler, more solid values. If he was aggressive, he also knew how to be independent. Bob didn't let the pressures of his work shunt him into the pursuit of totally frivolous people and values. He didn't feel he had to smoke, drink or go along with the crowd in those small ways that make some people feel more "in" socially. In short, Bob Green definitely was his own man.

Despite the expensive silk suits and brash manner, the real Bob, I soon saw, actually was quite sensitive and vulnerable—a real softie.

By now it wasn't hard to admit to myself that this man was everything I wanted, but I still couldn't believe the timing was right. I wasn't ready, I kept insisting, but all the time I was falling more deeply in love with him.

God's timing doesn't always coincide with ours. He knew Bob was ready for marriage, even if I felt I wasn't. Looking back on things now, I wonder how in the world I got him. Probably by seeming to be so aloof and hard to get, I imagine, which really was no act.

Here was Miami's most eligible bachelor, handsome, successful, well liked, a real swinger who cut a wide swathe among the girls—yet he selected an unsophisticated gal like Anita Bryant to fall for. I couldn't figure it out at the time. What did Bob Green see in me?

The answer was simple. The good-time girls, the real swingers, just weren't the type Bob had in mind as possible wife material. Like most other men, he wanted to establish a home with a wife who possessed high moral standards—the kind of woman he wanted to rear his children.

Thank goodness, I did stick to my standards. The fact that I did, that I obviously didn't compromise them even for someone glamorous, impressed Bob strongly.

Those girls who give themselves to the man they love before marriage really succeed in cheating themselves. I know and understand how strong the temptation is, but also I know something else: there is nothing else more beautiful and wonderful than sexual love between marriage partners—when that love is entered into and blessed by God. Why would anyone want to accept anything less?

As Bob and I considered marriage, we seemed to have an unusual number of obstacles to clear away. Several members of my big family just couldn't see Bob as being the right type man for me.

Bob, on the other hand, had plenty of show business friends who felt he was about to do the wrong thing. To others, we did not seem like a particularly compatible couple. People saw me as an open, uncomplicated young woman—all out on the surface. The real Bob Green, meanwhile, was hidden behind the sophisticated image which emerged from his career. No wonder we didn't appear to be right for one another!

Soon Bob arranged for me to meet his parents, Svea and Einar Green, who were natives of Sweden. They are citizens of the United States now, of course, and for years had lived in New York, in the Bronx where Bob grew up.

We all had dinner together at a very nice restaurant Bob had selected. You can imagine how self-conscious I felt, how nervous, even though these thoroughly sweet and cordial people did everything to make me feel at ease.

As the meal progressed, I gradually relaxed. Then Bob reached under the table and began to hold my hand. I really didn't appreciate that one bit. His parents had never met me before. What kind of girl would they think I was? Silently and indignantly, I tried to pull my hand away. Bob held firm, however, and there was nothing I could do about it without being obvious.

At last he released my hand. I sat up straight, glared at Bob, then turned to say something to his mother. But Mrs. Green wasn't looking at my face. As my eyes followed hers, we both gasped aloud. On the proper finger of my left hand, Bob had placed a ring with a large, beautiful, heart-shaped diamond!

Immediately, of course, all formality vanished. Bob's mother was hugging me, tears in her eyes, and his father had gotten to his feet to shake hands with Bob. It was a sweet, emotional moment, filled with the warmth Bob's family expresses so naturally.

Eventually it came time for me to leave the Breakfast Club and another important spot on the George Gobel TV

Show, so I could plan our wedding. Some of my friends were disappointed for me, leaving such good professional opportunities behind, but it had to be done. Nothing else would have worked. Like any other wife, I would have to go where my husband went.

Time moved closer to June 25, the date Bob and I had set for our wedding. We both were so busy, so separated from one another, and still there remained one vitally important issue for us to settle.

The fact was: Bob and I had not talked sufficiently about our religious faith. He knew about mine, of course, and I knew he understood and approved of the place I reserve for God in my life.

But what about Bob? Like many other Swedes, he had been reared in the Lutheran denomination, which I greatly respect. But Bob had not been saved; he frankly admitted to being just a nominal Christian, and even looked somewhat puzzled when I tried to explain what I meant by being saved through Christ.

Had God not stepped in and taken over, this could have been a terribly dangerous place in our relationship. As our wedding approached, I became more and more serious. Bob, always sensitive to what is happening inside me, could see that I was in the process of turning everything about our forthcoming life over to the Lord, for His blessing and protection.

Bob sensed the solemnity of this thing. The night before our wedding, we went to see our minister and then we talked with Gloria Roe, my close friend in Christ. Only three or four years older than I, she'd been my spiritual sister since I was a teen-ager in Tulsa. Gloria also is a fantastically gifted pianist and composer of sacred songs. She often accompanied me when I sang in public.

Gloria composed a special song for our wedding—that's the kind of friend she is.

I'll never forget the closeness among us as we knelt and asked God to bless our marriage. In a true sense, that commitment felt as deep and important as the actual ceremony to come.

As we talked—as Gloria gently drew Bob out about his Christian beliefs—something wonderful happened. The Spirit of God descended upon us. Bob felt led to confess Jesus Christ as his Lord and Saviour.

This came as the holiest, most amazing gift to our impending marriage. The radiance of that moment lingered through those final hours before our wedding, and started our life together in perfect joy.

Because I had been Miss Oklahoma, our wedding was well covered by the press. Station KAKC, which had sponsored me in the pageant, designated Saturday, June 25, 1960, as Anita Bryant Day. At noon, after Bob and I were married, it was changed to Mrs. Bob Green Day.

A wedding of two show business personalities seems highly newsworthy to the general public, I guess. However, the *real* news about us that day never made the papers.

I refer, of course, to the Gospel, the good news, which God sent to Bob and me at the very outset of our new life together.

11

Love and Conflict

Bob AND I CAUGHT a plane for New York immediately after the buffet reception which followed our wedding. In a way this trip almost seemed to symbolize the way our marriage has worked out, for we traveled not toward our honeymoon, but to a big show date.

Rehearsals for a television special called "Coke Time" were to begin the next day. I was to appear with Pat Boone, Bobby Rydell, Bobby Darin, Paul Anka, Annette Funicello, and other young recording artists within the top ten in popularity.

After the show on Monday the cast threw a very nice party for Bob and me, and then we left for our honeymoon at Dorado Beach, Puerto Rico.

Actually, we didn't mind beginning married life with work. Bob and I really like show business, understand its demands, and we know the only way you survive is to accommodate yourself to them.

Back home in Miami, Bob returned to his job at station WINZ while I became a . . . what? The Breakfast Club and the George Gobel Show were things of the past, of course. I gave up all television work when I married Bob. So now I was a housewife within a compact, beautifully furnished apartment which almost took care of itself.

Soon time began to hang unbearably heavy on my hands. As the weeks went by my records continued to do well, but otherwise my career just seemed to hang in limbo.

I needed something to do before everything I'd worked toward all my life ground to a dead halt. Meanwhile, I felt guilty for having such thoughts. *A new bride should content herself with home and husband,* I told myself. *What was wrong with me?*

Another goad toward working was the fact that Bob and I had spent our money recklessly on rings, trousseau, wedding, honeymoon, and long distance telephone calls. Bob's job certainly would support us just fine, but I felt I also needed to be contributing to the family coffers.

As Bob perceived my restlessness and discontent, he tried to help me.

"Why don't you take some of those night club dates your agency keeps trying to get you to fill?" he suggested. "At least it would give you something to do, and a certain visibility again."

I'd always resisted night club offers in the past. I just didn't feel I could work the club circuit and maintain a Christian testimony. Bob, on the other hand, as a new babe in Christ had no particular feelings about night clubs, so long as they were of a certain caliber.

So I went along with Bob against my own inner judgment, because I thought I should. Meanwhile, he didn't realize the conflict this set up within me.

That's why the first months of our marriage became almost the unhappiest period of our lives. For one thing, I had to travel. We both came to dread the separations, but neither felt free to talk to the other about it. I began to resent each club date fiercely, and each seemed worse to me than the one before. I was simply out of my element, and I knew it.

Naturally I took my resentments out on Bob. Poor man, he not only had to hold down a demanding job, but he had to handle the strains of adjusting to a new marriage for which there didn't seem to be any rule book.

At last we had to admit that our home life much of the time was worse than rough; it sometimes was hellish. What's more, Bob and I really loved one another. He sincerely wanted nothing but my happiness. If I wanted to continue to sing, he wanted me to have this. Also, Bob was unwilling to tell me what I could do or couldn't do for my career's sake. If I needed to travel, he let me go without a complaint. When I growled about the night club jobs, he listened without much comment.

So things rocked along, going from bad to worse. One day Bob got fed up.

"We've got to talk, Anita," he said. "If we don't do something pretty soon our marriage will go down the drain. I don't want to tell you what to do, of course, but I feel you should stop making these night club appearances. I see these are wrong for you."

How relieved I felt, when that was settled! Still, it didn't really stay settled long. I still needed work. Moodily, I imagined my performing life was coming to a close, that I'd become a has-been at age twenty. My disposition began to fluctuate between bad temper and despair.

Concurrently with this, Bob began to notice that I wasn't really the best business woman in the world. My financial affairs were in terribly poor shape, he sensed. Other things were pretty slipshod, too, and a good businessman like Bob couldn't help but see that some of my advisors were prone to take advantage of my youth and ignorance.

There was another problem, too—an old one with me. I was still headstrong and stubborn, while Bob's nature is easy-going and tolerant. Everything in me instinctively tried to boss Bob around, but he wasn't about to let me. Now Bob's no tyrant, but he has a strong personality. He's just not the sort of man who'll abdicate his authority as head of the household. That really would have meant the death of our marriage, and Bob knew it.

These stresses were silent, of course, and they were continual. I think two things caused our marriage to survive that first terrible year—our love for one another, and our mutual trust in God. Many times that year we had to get down on our knees together and plead with God to help our marriage.

That help came through the person of Henry Stone, a record distributor who had been Bob's best man when we got married. Henry is somewhat older than Bob, is an excellent businessman, and someone whose integrity you instinctively trust.

"Look kids, you two are acting crazy," Henry told us abruptly. "What you need to establish right now before you go any further is that you two need to be together if you want your marriage to work.

"Bob, you're not the type of guy who needs show business for some kind of ego-fulfillment thing. You got into the business rather late. You've been very successful, and you keep getting very good offers from the big networks and others.

"But Bob, you don't care about all that, and I know it. You know as well as I do, your greatest potential could be in managing Anita!"

It made so much sense from my standpoint that I had to hold my breath. Besides having a great musical background and knowing absolutely all the top artists and show business personalities, Bob's experience included radio and television, sportscasting, production and disc jockey work. He also was very knowledgeable about contractual matters, and in general knew most of the vital ropes in this complicated world we work in.

Henry's help came at exactly the right point in our marriage. Bob was proud of my career and wanted me to enjoy it, but he could see it getting out of hand. He didn't have the nerve to ask me to quit, but he thought I was being so badly mismanaged that it eventually could damage our marriage beyond repair. He saw me having trouble with bookings, contracts, fees, all the practical stuff I just wasn't really equipped to cope with.

To make our situation all the more delicate, Bob had begun to realize that he'd enjoy taking over the managing, but a strong sense of professional ethics prevented his suggesting such a thing. I, on the other hand, used to long for Bob to take over, but would never dare say a word for fear Bob would sacrifice his own professional future for me.

I knew Bob had every reason to go to the very top in his field. Why should he give up his career just so I could have mine? I felt ashamed to even dream of such a sacrifice. Also, though I knew he'd make a top-notch manager, I feared that being both husband and manager might just be too much.

Thank God for Henry Stone, who understood us both so well. As a disinterested third party he could kindly and succinctly point out the facts in a very objective way. And that's all it took. Bob and I felt a breathtaking degree of relief and delight as we agreed to enter a new partnership.

Secure in his feelings about his own manhood, Bob just

didn't have the need to maintain a place in the limelight. He values good work and is highly businesslike, but the fact is he'd rather work his heart out in behalf of my interests than work for somebody else and get more glory.

I saw this decision as a major piece of unselfishness on Bob's part. It came about because he placed our marriage and my happiness above anything he might want for himself.

It would be nice to say that everything straightened out immediately on the heels of our decision, but that simply wasn't so.

Actually, the next major stumbling block to recognize in our marriage was Anita Bryant Green. I gratefully accepted Bob's generous decision to manage my career, you see, but right away I started out by getting in his way.

It was that same old bossy streak, of course. After all, I'd overseen my affairs so long that I really thought I knew plenty well how to do it. Then too, Bob naturally made a mistake or two at first, and that made me critical.

We continued to have plenty of fights, but Bob wasn't about to let me walk over him. At last I realized I'd better turn this over to Bob, *really* turn it over to him, or he couldn't help me. And the only way I knew to do that was to try to turn my bossy nature over to God.

When I resorted to Christ, He helped me relinquish authority so my husband could assume proper control. This may be news to Bob, of course. He thinks I'm still plenty bossy!

Often Bob and I speculate as to how our marriage might have turned out had the first year been happier. Perhaps there'd have been less incentive to go into a career partnership in addition to a marital one. In that case, we'd have

missed some of the most rewarding parts of our life together.

More important, I wonder if we would have prayed together as much. Our miserable marriage often required
that we go down on our knees together. Despite ourselves,
the relationship began to draw strength from God's
strength, wisdom from God's wisdom.

We both know full well that God wanted Bob to take
over my career. When we began to follow His path for
us my faltering career began to zoom.

God, of course, could see that Bob would develop a
genius for the work he's doing. As the years go by, I become increasingly more amazed by my husband's rare
qualities of perception and creativity.

I don't deserve such a break, but God provided me with
a manager who's every bit as great as my husband. No performer could ask any more than that!

12

To Witness for God

THE NIGHT CLUB work about which I spoke so disparagingly turned out to be a prime lesson for Bob and me. Since I'd never done that type of work before I married, I didn't have any way of knowing that the hours and atmosphere just weren't for me. My mistake was that I went on my own and did this work without relying on Christ to provide the kind of bookings that would have been right for me. But maybe we needed to do it on our own in order to get so thoroughly unhappy that we'd have to turn our professional futures over to God.

Financially, night club work is very rewarding. Our unhappiness at last outweighed the money I was making, however, and we decided to turn down all such offers in the future. At that time we had no idea of what we might do instead.

From the moment Bob and I made that decision and stepped out on faith, good things began to happen. I had made a couple of commercials for the Coca-Cola Company, only a few, but right then and there they signed me to a long-term contract, which was an excellent break indeed. It meant a great deal more in terms of security, too. The relationship became very happy and wholesome, and we worked with Coca-Cola for seven years.

Too many other such good opportunities have come to us since then for the whole thing to be accidental. I'm convinced that when you turn your business over to God entirely, He not only will send you exactly the type work that's best for your talents and your nature, but He'll help you begin to aim higher, so your ambitions will become more worthy of Him.

It becomes a matter of really trusting the Lord to provide. This has to be learned. It may sound strange to those who don't operate the way Bob and I do, but we absolutely know the Lord will open all the right doors.

So far the results have been pretty spectacular for us. I've watched other pop singers continue to do the night club circuit as Bob and I, because of God's guidance, gradually settled into a unique type of life that actually involves a minimum of travel and time away from home as well as the kind of fees I never dreamed I'd command.

Lest this sound smug, let me hasten to say the path hasn't been entirely smooth. From our first year until now, Bob and I frequently argue about decisions. I'm not the type to sit back meekly and let him do it all, and he's not the type to let me horn in when I really don't understand the particulars. So we have our moments.

Some of these fusses revolved around, of all things, my Christian testimony! Soon after Bob started managing me, we changed record companies and I began to record for Columbia. One thing I really wanted to do was cut an album of sacred songs, something I'd never tried before.

Now I'd sung both pop songs and religious songs all my life, but I'd always kept the two things strictly apart. I never sang pop songs to religious audiences—nor did I sing sacred songs in a pop style, or to a pop audience. These were reserved for revivals and other religious programs. I always had kept the two kinds of music totally separate. I didn't believe in combining them.

Bob, on the other hand, thought perhaps I should. For example, there was the sacred album I wanted so much to do. Bob suggested that it might include a few songs that were not strictly hymns, so that it might reach a wider audience.

There was merit to his suggestion, but I needed to be convinced. For one thing, Bob admitted that sacred music was a whole new field to him, and he felt he really didn't know it very well. Our solution was to get together with Gloria Roe and our good friend Bruce Howe of the Rodeheaver Publishing Company. The four of us sat down together and considered possible titles.

What emerged was a mixed group, as Bob had suggested. "Abiding Love," one of Gloria's songs, became the title number. The album also included such old standards as "In The Garden," "Sweet Hour Of Prayer," and "How Great Thou Art."

Bob actually was responsible for bringing that album out of me. As he predicted, it did reach a far wider audience than we could have imagined. It became a sure, steady seller that continues to do well, and in so doing, gives my Christian testimony as I really wanted to do.

Now there's the catch: I had very definite opinions about how the Lord wanted me to give this testimony, and Bob disagreed with these. As Bob knew, all my life I had tried to *live* my testimony. I considered this to be a very personal thing, not something you got up in public and talked about. For example, I'd never speak about Christ to a youth group, unless it were in church, and I never mentioned Christ to a pop-type audience.

I wanted to keep the sacred world separate from the secular. Bob thought this was wrong.

When he told me I should be willing to testify anywhere to the power of Christ, I felt Bob wanted to infringe on my personal salvation. We'd have terrific arguments about this. I accused him of intruding on me, of trying to exploit something priceless, of wanting me to cheapen my faith. These were harsh accusations indeed!

"How can you say that, when the Bible tells you to go out and preach to all men?" Bob asked me. Or he'd say:

"Anita, who do you think *really* needs it? You're in one of the roughest, dirtiest, phoniest businesses in the world—show business. This is where you need to give your testimony. You could use it as a vehicle to really witness for Christ—if you're genuinely sincere about it.

"If you're not, Anita, then keep it to yourself. But if you're honest with yourself, if you really love Jesus, then say so."

It was hard to believe my ears. I literally had given a testimony through music all my life. Now here was Bob Green, a relatively new Christian, challenging me to begin using my entire professional life for this purpose: asking me to speak up for Christ. He really shook me up.

"Bob, you don't know how hard it would be for me to do this," I stammered. "It's easy for me to get up in public and sing a pop song, or get up in front of church and sing a sacred one, but to put those two images together . . . !

"For one thing, it really wouldn't be commercial. You're going to get a lot of people who won't want me on certain television shows because they're going to say, she's too religious, she's too fanatic, and all that. On the other hand, it could hurt my church image as much as the pop image," I insisted.

As frequently as this argument came up, we never seemed to resolve it. Sometimes the discussion got really personal and heated, and those times left me feeling quite hurt with Bob.

But if a Christian-marital-professional relationship can get terribly touchy at times, there also are some rewards you can't get any other way.

As my manager, Bob always travels with me. He's there to handle every detail of everything, from hailing taxis to negotiating contracts. In his calm way he really takes over and smooths the way for everything that needs doing—even straightens out a messed-up schedule when I disrupt things by sneaking in a little shopping on a New York business trip.

Before we had children we enjoyed traveling anytime we had a chance. I love to go places with Bob. Routine business trips became something out of the ordinary, events we both looked forward to. We didn't mind working our heads off. We were willing to work hard and travel hard, as long as we were together.

And as we worked hard together that way, we came to realize more and more how compatible we are; our personalities seem to balance. No doubt this is one reason Bob has guided my career into novel and somewhat daring channels at times. He knows me so well!

The sacred album, again, illustrates how we complement one another. It was my idea to do that album, because I felt a conviction about it. This was a labor of love, and Bob understood that completely. It would be the first time I offered my Christian testimony on a national scale.

After that, Bob began to chide me about my unwillingness to give my spoken testimony in the same way—freely, not weighing and measuring the audience who would receive it. I still picked and chose my groups pretty carefully, and Bob said this limited the affect of what I had to say.

Again and again, he reminded me that Christ told us to preach the gospel to all the world. I never had any answer for that. Since I knew Bob was right, it bugged me even more.

"My real testimony is through song," I continued to argue. "The album was a breeze because I've sung all those things all my life, and I feel them from the bottom of my heart. But Bob, I just don't speak all that well. I'm sorry."

Nothing I said convinced him. I just don't speak eloquently. Sometimes I have to grope for the words. I feel uneducated . . . inadequate . . . stupid. . . .

God solved our impasse in His usual ingenious way; eventually a commercial commitment led to my agreeing to do what Bob asked. As we'd travel to various cities on behalf of our business commitments, different churches began to invite me to sing, and to give a spoken testimony as well.

At first I resisted strongly. It scared me to death. I'd never talked before my own church. I'd always witnessed through my singing. But now, with Bob prodding me none too gently, I began to talk.

I began to tell people that I love Christ . . . what my faith means to me . . . how He sustains me with His strength. It was very simple and halting. Often I wondered if what I had to say could possibly mean very much to those who heard it.

Always, as I give my testimony, Bob sits close by me on the platform. I like his solid, comforting presence at a time like this. Sometimes too, to be honest, I fume a little inside and think, "Bob Green, you got me into this!"

It's a good thing that he did, however, because after a number of such appearances in various churches, I was asked to testify during a Billy Graham rally. This time I really did want to break and run.

There had been some incidents with the college kids on the beach at Fort Lauderdale, Florida a few years ago, and the city of Fort Lauderdale invited Dr. Billy Graham to come to the beach and speak to the kids.

Gloria Roe had appeared with Billy on many occasions and knew him well. She telephoned him to suggest that he might invite me to share his platform since I was a Christian who had a testimony, that I lived in nearby Miami and the kids might relate to me because of my pop records.

Billy liked the idea fine, so Gloria approached Bob about my doing this. Of course, Bob thought I should, but I said *no*. What if they threw beer cans at me, or booed me off the stage? I refused. I was adamant.

Bob has a way of getting my dander up and backing me up against a wall. He gets me so terrifically mad at him that I hate him for pushing me into a corner. He did that now.

"You're a hypocrite," Bob said. "You profess to have Christ in your life, but you won't profess Him in public, which Christ tells you to do."

Because I know he's right, and hate him for making me feel so bad about it, I end up doing what I'm so scared to do. This time I faced a tough audience; even Billy Graham felt that way. We stood on a platform built right on the beach, gazing out into a sea of cold young faces that seemed to stare right through us.

Though my courage faltered badly, I forged ahead. I gave my testimony, haltingly as usual, and then I sang.

The kids were reverent—really reverent. They listened to me attentively. Their faces reflected nothing, but they listened. I left the stage feeling that Bob was right, Gloria was right, and God had been able to use me.

Slowly, I began to capitulate on this thing. More and more often I came to the place where I could speak up for God. I honestly cannot say it ever gets much easier. Each time, I pray beforehand, *Lord, remove Anita Bryant from all this. I'm here to glorify You, Lord, not me. Please put Your words into my mouth, and let Your truth show forth to these people.*

He has used my simple testimony before business groups, youth assemblies, servicemen, conventions, and even White House dinners hosted by the President of the United States.

That's how good a manager my husband is. He willingly handles all the business in my life—even to including the Lord's business. Despite our sometimes violent scraps, I love him for it.

13

Bobby and Gloria

It can be devastating for a woman to learn that she perhaps may never bear children.

The news hit Bob and me particularly hard, for we'd both counted on having a house full of kids. Bob had been an only child and an only grandchild, and I had been crazy about babies all my life. Even after I was established in television and had precious little time of my own, I'd baby-sit free for friends just so I could take care of their babies.

My problem was a physical one which doctors hoped might respond to surgery. Carol Oshins, whose husband Milt is Henry Stone's partner, knew exactly how I felt, because she and I experienced similar frustrations.

"Adopt a baby," the Oshins advised us. "Don't wait to see whether or not you can have one by natural birth. Look at our beautiful daughter!"

We had been married three years by now, and Bob and I hated to wait much longer to start raising children. Working through a lawyer and an agency, we began the numerous tests and interviews required of prospective adoptive parents.

It seemed that only God could "match" us with a child.

Bob's background is pure Swedish, but I'm an all-American girl with French, Dutch, Scotch, Irish, English and one-eighth Cherokee Indian blood lines. How could any agency match that?

"Please try to get us a baby with Scandinavian ancestry," I told our case worker.

I felt it was terribly important that we find just the right child to carry on Bob's name. Obviously we'd find it next to impossible to adopt a newborn baby with my sort of heritage, but I hoped so much that God would lead us to one with Bob's. Meanwhile, through friends, we put out feelers in Sweden, Denmark and Norway. Surely, somewhere, there'd be a blond, blue-eyed baby for us!

In August, 1963 we received a stunning phone call from our lawyer.

"Congratulations! You can become parents, if you wish. The baby will be born in September," he said.

It all sounded much too good to be true. The parentage of the unborn child was excellent, their circumstances highly unusual. The baby not only would match Bob's background, but to an astonishing extent would even match mine. And whoever heard of finding an adoptive baby so promptly?

It seemed as though our prayers had been answered to perfection. We could become parents in only three weeks!

Suddenly I got cold feet.

"Bob, I just don't know. What kind of mother is a show business mother? All that travel and hard work. I'd have to leave the child alone sometimes. Maybe I don't have the right temperament for motherhood; maybe that's why God hasn't let us give birth."

Patiently, Bob heard my fears out. In the end, we met them as we meet every other family crisis—on our knees.

Night after night Bob and I prayed to know God's will about accepting the child who seemed to be so right for us. Our own emotions were so mixed, fear and yearning and hope and more fear, that we could not seem to make a sensible choice.

And the deadline was so close! We had to let the lawyer know our intentions. We couldn't keep everyone dangling. Suddenly, one day, we just knew.

"We do want the baby," Bob told our lawyer over the telephone.

"Of course you do," came the calm reply. "Everybody does some soul searching toward the last, but I knew you'd want it.

"By the way, are you hoping for a boy or for a girl?"

That hardly seemed important to us. Like most other parents, we just wanted a healthy baby. "I'd prepare for a daughter if I were you," the lawyer advised us jocularly. "For some reason, every adoption I've handled for the past couple of years has involved a baby girl."

It didn't matter to us. Excitedly, Bob and I rushed out and bought the thousand and one things it takes to equip a nursery. Other couples have months in which to dream and prepare. We had days—days sandwiched between professional engagements, at that.

We were at one of these bookings, lunching with rodeo officials at Pine Bluff, Arkansas, when I was called to the telephone. Our lawyer's secretary was on the line.

"Mrs. Green, I'm happy to inform you that you just became the mother of a seven pound, one ounce son!"

I felt stunned. "A boy? Are you sure it's a boy?" It took a moment to adjust. I had accepted the lawyer's casual prediction that we'd have a daughter.

Thoroughly elated, Bob and I flew home immediately.

Just as other parents do, we took little Robert Einar Green, Jr. home from the hospital when he was five days old. And just like many other first time parents, we felt shook when we saw him.

Bobby was an unusually long baby—twenty-three inches —and he seemed terribly scrawny to us. His face was red, his body wrinkled, and his nose seemed to spread across his face. In short, he looked just about like any other newborn infant, though Bob and I didn't know it. We had seen older, plumper babies, and that's what we expected. Still, neither of us wanted to let on to the other that we thought there might be anything about our son that was less than perfect.

"I love you, even if you aren't beautiful," I said as I kissed the top of his little head.

"He *is* beautiful," Bob said loyally.

That night I slept on the sofa in the Florida room with our son. He was scared and I was scared, and I'll never forget our first long night together as long as I live. Carol Oshins came over to admire him and teach me how to change his diapers. That was about the extent of my training for motherhood!

Little Bobby crept into our hearts immediately. Bob and I couldn't imagine how we had lived without this tiny blond mite who could bellow so savagely when his bottle was slow in coming.

Typically overconscientious, I tried to rear Bobby by the book. The baby cried a lot, so I consulted the book often. Now I know, of course, that he cried because I was tense, and I was tense because he cried. I should have thrown the book away and simply cuddled him, but I didn't know that then.

Instead, I walked the floor with him, fretted, sang to him, walked some more—and got terribly tired. Indeed, even after Bobby had been with us a while and began to settle into some semblance of a routine, I still felt tired and depressed, and sometimes even ill. About the time we took Bobby for his first check-up I decided I'd better have a check-up too.

"Sounds like you're pregnant," the doctor said.

I didn't find that funny. "Please, doctor, no jokes. Some other time, not now. Much as I would like to give birth some day, now is not the time."

But he was right, of course. What incredible news to take to Bob!

Bob was delighted. I was . . . well, mixed-up.

"If I thought I had mixed emotions before we got Bobby, I really do now," I told my husband. "How could God permit such confusion?

"I just want to learn to be a good mother to Bobby. It takes time to learn how to care for a tiny baby . . . and now this. It doesn't seem fair to him, Bob, for us to have another baby so soon!"

Nevertheless, that's exactly what God meant for us to do. Bobby was only seven and one-half months old when his baby sister was born the following May. Tiny Gloria Lynn, who we named for our dear friend, Gloria Roe, turned out to be as blonde as her brother, though she has dark brown eyes like mine.

Our first year with those two new babies was more hectic, and sometimes funnier, than I can tell you. No matter how rugged it all got, though, traveling with two diaper pails and all the rest of it, Bob and I still never lost sight of one thing: God's planning is perfect, even if ours isn't.

Because of His perfect timing, Bobby came to us, and

he, our first child, surely could not have been meant for any other home. The sweet, frolicky little boy with the sunny hair and shining smile seems to echo Bob in looks and disposition. We could not do without him.

And how good that Gloria Lynn turned out to be a girl—a great companion for her brother, but not quite the pesky competition that a brother might have meant to Bobby. From the first, Gloria Lynn has loved and looked up to him, and always he has cared for her.

Often people wonder if our first son and daughter are twins. They resemble one another closely. Only the facts of their births differ: one child was chosen, the other accepted. Both, however, were prayed for, and both represent their parents' answered prayers.

We always called Bobby and Gloria our miracle babies. We might have other children in the future, Bob and I told ourselves, but their coming would be far less dramatic.

Little did we know.

14

Putting Down Roots

MIAMI, to my small-town way of thinking, wasn't exactly the place I would have chosen for us to live and raise our children. Miami Beach in particular looked to me to be too swinging a place, a good-time town meant for adults, with little of the old-fishing-hole kind of fun for kids I remembered from my own childhood.

But none of this did I mention to Bob. When I married him I married Florida too, in a sense, because Bob and his parents had moved down there from the Bronx fifteen years earlier. Bob knew and loved the state, and understood the people, and I loved Bob; so that was that.

When we first were married we lived in an apartment. Several months later we began buying our own home, investing in good furniture, and putting down roots. We traveled a lot in those days, worked hard, had a lot of fun, and began to make money. Then the babies came and, like all other parents everywhere, we immediately began to reassess many of our values.

What did we want for these children? How would we live? What would we teach them? What would the Green family be like?

Looking back to the little towns like Tishomingo,

Oklahoma, where Sandy and I grew up, it seemed to me that we had wonderful childhood experiences. We were poor, sure, by today's standards of affluence. For that matter, Bob never had too much either in the way of material goods.

Then he and I worked our way up in a business which can be very rewarding financially. We could afford to give our children many of the advantages we hadn't known in our own childhood days—a beautiful home in a well-to-do neighborhood, private school.

"I keep thinking of Grandpa Berry, the way he'd take Sandra and me fishing with him," I told Bob one day. "I'd give anything if our kids could have that kind of experience.

"The freedom of it! Sandy and I thought the whole world belonged to us. I still remember how it felt to walk barefoot through the woods, clutching Grandpa's hand, heading for our favorite fishing hole. It was just about the most beautiful spot you ever saw.

"Instead of that, our kids have a swimming pool and a cabin cruiser docked behind the house on Biscayne Bay. Of course I feel grateful, Bob, for the things we have. At the same time, though, I wish our kids could know the simple life we knew."

The great thing about Bob is, he does understand. Before we were married I never could have foreseen how family-oriented he'd become and what a terrific husband and father he'd turn out to be.

"The career is fine, but it's just a means to an end," Bob often tells me. "It's business, Anita. We both enjoy our business; it's important to us. But the thing we're working for is this home of ours and all the lives in it. They're more important than anything else."

Fortunately, Bob always has kept this idea in focus. Not many other husbands in his position would suggest traveling with small children, for example. It was Bob who, knowing how both of us dreaded being separated from our babies, thought of taking one child with us whenever we made an out-of-town trip.

At first we tried taking both, but that didn't work too well. Then we let Bobby and Gloria take turns going with Mommie and Daddy, and that worked fine. One reason was, neither one really minded being left behind, thanks to Farmor and Farfar, Bob's parents.

Farmor means "father's mother" and *Farfar* means "father's father" in Swedish. Farmor and Farfar Green live in Boynton Beach, Florida, not too far from us, and they have literally made our way of life possible. Whenever business requires Bob's and my attention, they move in and become substitute parents for our children, who adore them.

Lucky as we are in that respect, Bob's main concern in managing me is to try to cut our travel time to a minimum. This he has done to an amazing degree. As the years go by he becomes increasingly more adept at scheduling more and more work for us within fewer and fewer absences from home. Meanwhile, he has built up quite a good career within a very home-centered framework.

For example, as a Christian, Bob automatically screens out any offers that could compromise our family's testimony in any way. Because we have children, he aims toward anything that will witness to youth or boost young people, and we accept only wholesome, family-type appearances.

"You can't work just for the dollar," Bob says. "Your work is part of your witness. It shows what kind of person you are, and what you stand for."

Bob also believes that a Christian should tithe his time and labors, as well as his money.

We didn't acquire all these values overnight, of course. Looking back, I believe they began during those first difficult months of marriage, when it seemed sometimes as though we wouldn't make it.

We used to pray together in the evenings occasionally then—not regularly, by any means, but sometimes. Bob was new in Christ. While I considered myself rather an old hand that way, I still had quite some growing to do—much more than I knew then!

We did grow. Fortunately, from those weak beginnings the seeds of our marriage began to sprout. Those days were rough, no doubt about it. Still, Christ was able to take our little unformed marriage and show us the way to better, stronger growth as the months and years went by.

Going to church on Sundays is one way we keep our family life centered where it should be. We think it's unusual the way the Lord led us to the Northwest Baptist Church here in Miami where we worship. This was early in our marriage, and we were visiting churches throughout the city, seeking the one that would be best for us. Bob and I were a little doubtful that we could find many Southern Baptists in Miami—we thought they were all in Oklahoma.

One Sunday morning as we hunted a particular church we got very lost. "We're going to be late, and I can't stand that," I told Bob. "Let's just enter the first Baptist church we see."

Minutes later we found one. Brand new, still without a sanctuary, the Northwest Baptist congregation worshiped inside a huge Quonset hut. The moment we entered, Bob and I noticed a special atmosphere. Nearly every individual there held a Bible in his hands. They were singing, so freely and joyously that I felt a thrill. Obviously the Holy Spirit moved among that congregation in full force.

The years since simply continue to reinforce our first impressions of what was to become our family's church. But even that first Sunday, Bob and I knew we were at home. The people were friendly, unpretentious, and wonderfully enthusiastic. The Rev. Homer Lindsay, Jr. preached a powerful sermon.

"So many churches these days aren't preaching the Word and aren't preaching Christ," I told Bob later. "You can tell Northwest Baptist has Christ as its nucleus. Those people really feel burdened for lost souls."

Bob felt this too. Soon I transferred my church letter and we both joined this magnificent congregation. On November 3, 1963, Bob was baptized there and became a member by his profession of faith.

We began to make a serious effort to build a Christ-centered family. Saying grace at meals was one way. Bobby and Gloria take turns blessing the food. And then there's family prayer, in addition to the prayers each of us says daily. Thank God we formed those habits early. The day was to come when our little family had to cling desperately to God to sustain us through great need.

But in those days, as we began doing the things which are habitual in good American homes everywhere, Bob and I didn't know about that. We simply knew our home would seem far from normal unless we let God stabilize it. In show business, it's easy to get off course. It's always easy to be led astray by money, publicity, glamour or dozens of other temptations.

Yes, I've been tempted too. Take this business of "image." I've seen pop singers who feel they must move from one groovy, swinging image to another, changing with the styles, always keeping an eye out for any publicity angle they can play.

Well, it's understandable. Publicity is the lifeblood of show business survival, in a way. It can be hard to exercise good judgment about it.

That's why I find it easiest to try to use Christ's standards in everything I do—even right down to costumes and makeup—in order to avoid getting the wrong kind of image. It saves a lot of bother, really. I never have to go into long-winded explanations as to why I won't use risqué lines in my act, or wear sexy costumes.

Still, it's not always easy to know exactly where to draw the line. Fortunately or unfortunately, Bob has most decided ideas about how I should dress.

"That just doesn't look like you, Anita," he'll say, when maybe I've changed my makeup somewhat more than he likes.

Sometimes I rebel and accuse him of wanting me to look forever like the girl next door—about as exciting as vanilla ice cream. But of course Bob never tells me what to do. I may fuss and fume and argue for a while, but I always end up by accepting his opinion.

I'm glad I do. When I think about it, some of the best things about our life have come about from my listening to Bob.

It's Bob who guided my energies into such a breadth of appearances; family-type things like rodeos, summer stock, state fairs, and business conventions. There are our popular and sacred recordings, each of which has enjoyed a wonderful success. But something surprising (that neither of us could have foreseen) has turned out to be the backbone of the whole Bob-Anita venture.

That's the really great opportunity we've had of be-

Mother, Daddy and me. *Left:*
Daddy holds me and Mother
holds Sandra the year I was
three.

Sandra Jean and me. *Below:* On the left, I had just been named Miss Oklahoma. Dolly Hoskins, right, who ran the Miss Oklahoma pageant, accompanied me to New Jersey as my official chaperone during the Miss America Pageant.

Second from the left, I was among the top five finalists in the Miss America contest, and I became the second runner-up in the pageant. *Right:* Bob Green, of Miami Radio Station WINZ, was one of America's top ten disc jockeys and I was a 19-year-old singer whose second record had just climbed past the one million sales mark when we met in Miami.

Our wedding picture includes, from the left, Einar and Svea Green (Farfar and Farmor), Daddy (Warren Bryant), Mother and Daddy George (Leonora and George Cate). *Right:* Bob and I enjoyed those first hectic years of traveling and working together. Before the babies came, we were on the road twelve months of the year.

I like to sing Country and Western music, and like to play rodeos. *Below:* In Viet Nam, Dr. Billy Graham gave a Christmas message to the troops: John 3:16.

With Bob Hope and General William Westmoreland in Viet Nam. *Right:* Command performances for the King and Queen of Thailand were exciting landmarks in three of the Bob Hope tours. With the Queen, and Mr. Hope.

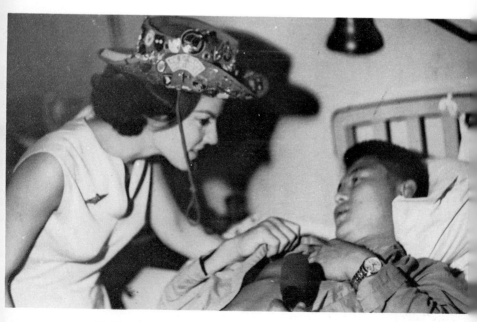

Visiting a wounded soldier at Nah Trang, Viet Nam.

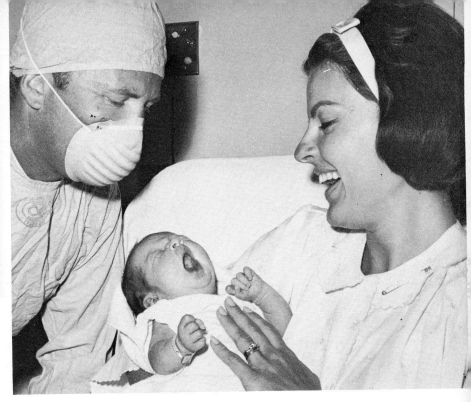

Bob and me with baby Gloria. *Below:* Because of the Bob Hope Holiday Tours, Bob and I celebrated Christmas on New Year's Day with little Gloria and Bobby.

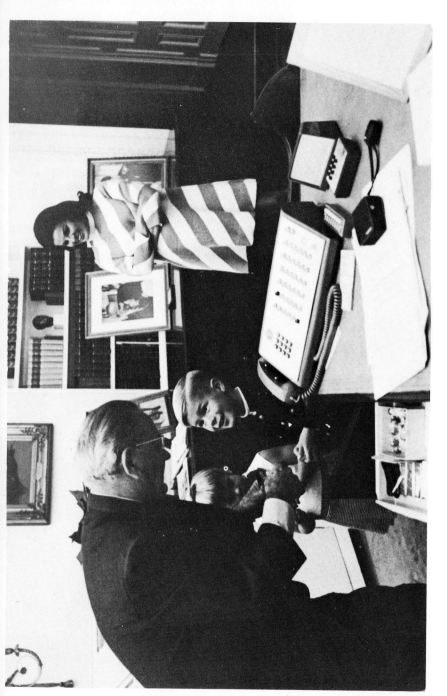

President Lyndon Baines Johnson, Gloria and Bobby and me at the White House.

coming a sort of spokesman for certain American industries. There was The Coca-Cola Company, in the first instance, the Florida citrus industry at present, and others such as Kraft Foods, Friedrich Air Conditioners, the Tupperware people, and the Holiday Inns of America, Incorporated, who have held equally valued places in our lives.

Where else in show business could a Christian give a witness on stage and sing such songs as "How Great Thou Art" and "Mine Eyes Have Seen the Glory"? These fine American companies aren't afraid to speak out for God and country. This is the wholesome, constructive kind of work God led us into when we became willing to trust Him with our lives.

As a performer, I don't have to be told how important television exposure is. So it's especially gratifying for us to know we can turn down offers to appear on shows that don't meet God's standards—and still be seen by millions of people on commercials and on family shows like the Lawrence Welk Show, Kraft Music Hall, the Orange Bowl Parade and others.

Dick Shack, a topflight artist's agent with the Agency for the Performing Arts, arranges our bookings, but it's Bob who oversees the myriad details that keep our business running smoothly. He keeps me home with the children every possible minute, while he works out the logistics of our lives. Bob also handles my personal publicity. That way we can know that every word that goes out is absolutely honest. We have a horror of phony publicity stories.

15

Americans Abroad

For YEARS, as I've said, Bob has worked hard for our family's sake to cut our traveling to a minimun. But there are some 300,000 miles he and I shared that we wouldn't take back for anything.

I mean the world-famous Bob Hope Holiday Tours to the armed forces stationed in remote outposts overseas, made on behalf of the U.S.O.

"Go with us one time, Anita, and it will get into your blood," Bob Hope suggested in 1960, the first year Bob and I were married. "You'll never play to a greater audience."

Spend our first Christmas away from home! I gulped and my heart sort of fell at the suggestion, yet somehow Bob and I found ourselves doing just that—the first of seven consecutive Christmases we'd spend with Mr. Hope and the rest of his troupe, and hundreds of thousands of American servicemen stationed in various far-flung places around the globe.

How do you describe experiences like those?

Bob and I never have been able to convey adequately the feelings of pride that overwhelm us when we meet these Americans, wherever they are. We traveled with Mr. Hope's troupe to the Caribbean, the Arctic, the Pacific and the Near and Far East.

Christmas came to mean the "hot season" for the Green family. There was the Yule we spent at Guantanamo Bay, for example, the year of the crisis there, when our Christmas tree was a pineapple decorated with candy; and a more recent one, in Viet Nam, where we arrived in Saigon just moments after an explosion near our hotel killed several servicemen and severely wounded many others.

Mr. Hope's tours always involved three weeks of travel, entertaining, and the kind of person-to-person contact between G.I. and entertainer that you remember forever.

Except for that part of the tour that was taped for television use as the "Bob Hope Christmas Special," we donated our time to the troops. This is a somewhat difficult and expensive thing for an entertainer to arrange (three weeks during the holiday season) but my husband and I never questioned whether or not we should. We could not help but think of the thousands of American servicemen who give up much more than their time, efforts and Christmases at home, for us.

Each year, undeniably, it got harder for us to leave home. I cried to leave our babies, even under the splendid care of Farmor and Farfar, as we set off for our long trips to the other side of the world.

But that would be the last of the tears. From then on we Greens were a team with but one thought in mind: to reach out to every G.I. we could see, to thank him, shake his hand, encourage him and, I hoped, brighten his lonely Christmas just a bit.

Usually, however, the officers and troops did more for us than we could possibly do for them. They knocked themselves out to provide anything they thought we might need, from makeshift dressing rooms to their own scanty supply of fresh fruit. They'd wait hours in the rain so as to get a good seat for the show. No wonder Bob wrote down so many names and addresses, so we could contact various men's wives and mothers when we returned to the States.

I accompanied Bob Hope on his Holiday Tours more than any other female performer ever did, so he awarded me the title of "Den Mother." In 1963, when I was pregnant with Gloria, we decided nevertheless to make the long, rough trip anyhow. I'd never do such a thing today, but at the time the tour seemed too important to set aside.

The last three tours abroad with Bob Hope took my husband and me to Viet Nam. There was distinct danger these times, and more than once Bob and I discussed the wisdom of our flying together so much. With two small children to consider, we knew we should not take unnecessary risks.

Still, something continued to draw us on, as Bob Hope had said it would. That something is the incredible courage and stamina of the American fighting man, and still more, respect for all the good and decent things he stands for as an individual.

We soon learned that these men wanted good, wholesome entertainment, not just cheap laughs. They wanted to look at a real woman from back home, not just what Bob Hope called the "sexpot type." And Bob and I soon learned that these men, who often lived and worked just moments away from death, very much cared about God.

You sense a strong sense of mission among the fighting men in Viet Nam, an enormous compassion for all victims of Communist atrocities, especially the children, and a religious conviction that surely must resemble the "faith of our fathers."

On Christmas Eve, we traditionally closed our show with my leading the cast and troops in singing "Silent

Night." Always, afterwards, I'd cry my eyes out. There in Viet Nam, in the muddy, battle-scarred camps where we played to jam-packed audiences, "Silent Night" became one of the most poignant and meaningful songs I ever delivered to any audience.

I can close my eyes now and see some of those faces. Always, as I looked at them through a blur of tears, I wondered how many of them would never see another Christmas.

The Road to Viet Nam, and to the other important places Mr. Hope visits at Christmas, had to end for Bob and me after the 1966 trip. That year Bobby and Gloria became old enough to understand that Daddy and Mommie were gone quite a few days. They cried for us a lot, Farmor and Farfar said, and really seemed to suffer from our absence.

"Anita, I think it's time we decide to spend Christmas at home," Bob said gently.

We were quiet for a bit, remembering this and that: Christmas Eve in a Saigon hotel room, where we spread our children's pictures out on the bed and reminisced about home . . . the U.S. Army major who had thanked us for coming to Viet Nam at Christmas, saying, "I know how it is to leave your children, ma'am. I have five kids of my own" . . . the young sergeant we met in a mess hall in Cu Chi, who proudly showed us pictures of his firstborn son, whom he'd never seen . . . the tears in the eyes of those rugged Green Beret guys as they joined me in singing, "Glory, glory, hallelujah" . . . Billy Graham's Christmas message to the troops from the Book of John, Chapter 3, verse 16: "For God so loved the world, that He gave His only begotten Son, that whosoever believeth in Him should not perish, but have everlasting life."

So it wasn't easy to decide. By Thanksgiving, 1967, we still had not made any really final decision about whether or not we'd return for another tour of Viet Nam. Bob and I thought back to the previous Thanksgiving, when I sang for troops at Fort Leonard Wood, Missouri, America's largest training post. Many of the men in that audience were in Viet Nam by now, I knew.

I had sung to them with a full heart indeed. After the show, Bob and I went to the post hospital to receive half of the stiff quota of innoculations we had to take before we could travel overseas.

"By the way, I'd like to get a fatigue jacket to wear in Viet Nam," I'd told one of our military escorts. I meant, of course, that I'd like to buy one, if possible. I had collected dozens of military patches and other insignia from the various outfits I'd visited, and I meant to attach these to the jacket and wear it overseas. The ranger hat I'd "collected" already was heavy with my trophies.

"I intend to cover that jacket with patches," I told Bob. "I want every outfit over there to be well represented."

Before we left Fort Leonard Wood that day I got my fatigue jacket, all right. To my astonishment, it had my name stencilled above the left breast pocket: BRYANT. It was to be more than a year before Bob and I learned the rest of that story.

The jacket belonged to a sergeant named Leon Bryant of Carbondale, Illinois. Later his hometown newspaper carried the story: how Sergeant Bryant came in from a three-week field problem, dirty . . . how the post photographer snapped his picture in the jacket before he even had a chance to wash his face . . . how the garment was given to Miss Anita Bryant for her use in Viet Nam.

How did I learn all that? Mrs. Yvonne Bryant, the sergeant's wife, mailed me the newspaper story along with a nice letter from Illinois.

"When you get to Viet Nam, please look up Leon," she asked. In the newspaper article Sergeant Bryant, asked what he'd like me to give him in exchange for his jacket, had said "a kiss on the cheek." I resolved to look him up and deliver that kiss.

Nevertheless, Bob and I reluctantly decided that we'd not be going to Viet Nam that year. Yvonne Bryant evidently read something to that effect in the newspapers, and she felt moved to write me a letter.

" . . . If you ever feel like disposing of Leon's jacket, I would be glad to have it. He died in Viet Nam November 14, 1967, from gunshot wounds received while on combat operations when hit by hostile small arms fire . . . Leon was carrying a machine gun at the time and one of the members of his squad was pinned down by a V.C. . . . Leon moved forth trying to save his buddy that was being attacked by Viet Cong, while all the members of his squad safely took cover . . . Leon did save the life of his buddy, but the V.C.'s fired upon Leon, killing him instantly. . . ."

Bob and I felt sick—utterly stricken. It was like learning of the death of someone we had known intimately. It hurt to learn that Leon Bryant had a newspaper clipping about the jacket, and a letter from me in his pocket when he died. As I imagined the young man who once wore that jacket, I almost felt the weight of it, heavy now with insignia, across my shoulders.

What can one say at a time like that? Nothing. Absolutely nothing, yet I felt led to try to reach Yvonne Bryant by telephone—to try in my own halting way to express our sorrow for her sorrow.

This was not easy to do. Ultimately the trail led to

Yvonne's hometown newspaper editor, who relayed to us the information that she was living at that time with her parents. Since we didn't know her maiden name, that seemed to end our search.

A week later, our call was completed. Yvonne Bryant, hearing of our attempts to reach her, had telephoned us. She and her sergeant were newlyweds and had lived together only a few months before he left for Viet Nam.

Her voice was clear and young and steady.

"Leon was a Christian," she told me. "It's all right. He was proud to fight for his country. We had talked about this, about how it might happen, and he told me how he felt. Leon said he didn't mind dying for America. And Anita, Leon died a Christian. I know he is with Our Lord."

I shall never forget Yvonne Bryant's calm young voice. I had called to offer her comfort, but she had consoled me. In a way, this story represents for Bob and me so many others—small incidents and big events, each in its own way haunting—that Bob and I carry in our hearts.

Years earlier, before the Miss America Pageant, Toni Spencer said my world was too small. In less than a decade I had traveled an incredible number of miles across the length and breadth of the USA, and to more military bases on foreign soil than I can enumerate.

In all these places, Bob and I felt humbled by the greatness of America, as we saw it reflected from hundreds of thousands of faces of our fighting men abroad.

16

"Mine Eyes Have Seen the Glory...."

IF ANY ONE SONG could be said to demonstrate to me the awesome directness of God's force in my life, it would have to be the "Battle Hymn of the Republic."

There are several obvious reasons for this.

"Battle Hymn," as some people recall, is what I sang when, as *Variety* reported, I received the first standing ovation in White House history. Later when I again sang the hymn at the White House, I was to become the first performer ever to win two standing ovations there.

When Dr. Billy Graham and I became the first Americans ever to appear on the podiums of both the Republican and the Democratic national conventions (in 1968) each time there was a standing ovation as I sang "Battle Hymn of the Republic."

I have sung this hymn with the same effect to thousands of fighting men in Viet Nam. Indeed, wherever I appear and to whatever audience I sing it, "Battle Hymn" always seems to move people. It brings them to their feet. Sometimes it makes them cheer or weep.

Why should this be so?

I never have sung any other song that moves people in this way, nor do I expect to. But there's a story behind the

"Battle Hymn" and me, a story that involves many other people as well. I think it's something of a modern day parable which illustrates how, if we'll only obey Him, the Lord can take something as commonplace as a familiar hymn and make it touch human lives with a brilliant new light.

It all started several years ago, as Bob and I polished our show in preparation for a big convention. We wanted to update and improve our act, and we were looking for a new closing number.

The closing song always is the most important one. Everything builds toward that, and it provides the take-away the audience wants. I'd always closed with "He's Got the Whole World in His Hands." That's tender, yet exuberant, and expresses something wonderful about God's love. It shows what Bob and I believe as Christians. There's a definite message there.

Though we liked our closing number, still we searched for something with even more impact. We wanted to show our faith, and the place of Christ in our lives. After entertaining people throughout our act, we reasoned, it was time to give them something to take with them. Why not show them we're something more than *just* entertainers?

We were talking with Jim Beers, a business friend. "Anita, I just got back from Salt Lake City, where I heard the famous Mormon Tabernacle Choir," he told me. "When they closed their concert with the 'Battle Hymn of the Republic' they got a standing ovation.

"It was really thrilling," he went on, "and I immediately thought, 'There's only one other singer that could do that song, and do it well,'" Jim said. "Why don't you add it to your act?"

I just gave him a hard stare. "Well, thanks," I said rather

shortly. "So you think my mouth is as big as the whole Mormon choir!"

Everybody laughed, except Bob. He looked thoughtful. "You're right, Jim," he said. "It would be a great closing number."

"Ah, you two are nutty," I told them. I was thinking, of course, of the big, choral, massed sound which Jim had heard. How could any one individual give it that kind of impact? But Bob evidently heard something quite different in his head. Immediately he was sold on the idea of "Battle Hymn."

"You ought to think about it," Bob said. So I did. I'm learning to take his advice about things like this. The next day we mentioned the hymn to Chuck Bird, our arranger and conductor, and asked him to order the music so the three of us could study it. Chuck looked surprised.

"What a coincidence," he said. "Last night as I drove across the causeway I listened to a male solo recording of the 'Battle Hymn of the Republic' on the car radio. I immediately thought, 'What a great closing number that would be for Anita.' "

Bob and I just looked at one another. We were beginning to feel . . . something. Evidently Chuck had gotten his idea at the very time the night before when Jim, Bob and I were discussing the song.

"Let's go to the music room, boys, and look up that hymn," I said abruptly. I reached for our biggest hymnal, which is seven inches thick, because I felt sure it would include the number we wanted. I poked my finger into someplace around the middle of the book, flipped over the big pages, and . . . would you believe it opened to "Battle Hymn"?

Again, we all just looked at one another.

These little things continued to happen. As the three

of us began to work with the music, what we should do with it somehow just fell into place. It was as though God planted the same ideas in each of us, simultaneously. Our best arrangements always come about when the three of us work together that way, but never before had anything else gone so well.

There are times when the three of us work for a week or two on a single idea. Sometimes we worry with something over the course of months. This music, however, just fell into place immediately.

It seemed to Chuck, Bob and me that the old hymn should be presented in an entirely new way, as we'd never heard it done before. We decided to start it very slowly and simply, then steadily, gradually, let it build in power until it soared to a majestic climax.

As we worked, we had no difficulty in agreeing on which verses we'd use, how long the arrangement should be, or how many choruses we needed. As he worked at orchestrating the score, Chuck said, the arrangement just seemed to reveal itself to him. Bit by bit, it all worked out.

And as it worked itself out, each of us marveled at how much this hymn expressed our feelings about God, about our American troops, and so many other things that seemed fantastically timely and right. The song fit into everything we stood for.

"Let's debut 'Battle Hymn' for the big convention," Bob and Chuck proposed, and I agreed. Seldom had I felt so right about a number. I felt in my bones that this was our song.

As we rehearsed before opening night, each of us got increasingly more excited. "Chuck, you've outdone yourself with these arrangements," Bob told him. I agreed. About that time, a company official approached us.

"You're not thinking of doing the 'Battle Hymn' for this occasion, I hope?" he queried in a worried voice.

"Why certainly. It's the climax of our show," I told him. "Everything leads up to it!"

There was a silence, and my heart began to sink. Our friend mentioned the fact that we were down South, and among southerners—and that was a northern song. He was right, of course, but that never had occurred to us. "Battle Hymn of the Republic," composed during the Civil War, helped to inspire Union troops to victory. But that was a century ago. Who was thinking of the Civil War now?

"You'll find 'Battle Hymn' in all the hymn books," I told him. "It's a Christian hymn. With all the war in Viet Nam, that hymn sounds completely contemporary. Listen to the words!"

BATTLE HYMN OF THE REPUBLIC

Mine eyes have seen the glory of the coming of the Lord;
He is trampling out the vintage where the grapes of wrath
  are stored;
He hath loosed the fateful lightning of His terrible, swift
  sword;
  His truth is marching on.

Chorus

Glory, glory, hallelujah! Glory, glory, hallelujah!
Glory, glory, hallelujah! His truth is marching on.

He has sounded forth the trumpet that shall never call
  retreat;
He is sifting out the hearts of men before His judgment-
  seat:

O, be swift, my soul, to answer Him! be jubilant, my feet!
Our God is marching on.

Chorus

Glory, glory, hallelujah! Glory, glory, hallelujah!
Glory, glory, hallelujah! His truth is marching on.

In the beauty of the lilies Christ was born across the sea,
With a glory in His bosom that transfigures you and me;
As He died to make men holy, let us die to make men free,
While God is marching on.

Chorus

Glory, glory, hallelujah! Glory, glory, hallelujah!
Glory, glory, hallelujah! His truth is marching on.

Julia Ward Howe

As Bob and I headed back to grab some rest before
show time, we felt real concern about our closing number.
What if they asked us not to sing it? The whole act would
fall flat. My stubborn Indian streak began to rise.

"I know it will be good. I *know* what people's reactions
will be," I told Bob. "This is just something I feel. We've
got to do that song."

"Don't worry about it," Bob said at last. "We're going to
do it, that's all. They won't try to stop us." But I could see
he was somewhat worried.

By the time we reached home, I knew what I must do.
"I'm going to pray about the 'Battle Hymn'," I told Bob.
I went down on my knees.

Lord, I feel so strongly that you want us to do this hymn
for this particular audience. Something is trying to block
it. If it's your will for us to perform "Battle Hymn," please
remove whatever obstacles block our way.

As I got to my feet again, things suddenly felt right again.

I really felt led to do that song, and I knew the Lord would intervene on our behalf if it were His will that we close with "Battle Hymn."

That night the Hymn evoked from a predominately Southern audience a real ovation. God's message superseded any thoughts of sectionalism, and the words to a classic American hymn suddenly seemed to sing with a new authority. For me, it was a thrilling time indeed.

After that, "Battle Hymn" closed every act for our every audience. It never fails to have its effect. In fact, it even moved the Buddhists, when I sang for the King and Queen of Thailand three different years during the Bob Hope Christmas Tours. Always it seems to speak to people and oddly enough, it never gets old to Chuck, Bob and me. Though we've done it thousands of times by now, the music invariably creates a certain excitement within us as well as in the audience. No other number makes us feel that way.

In the fall of 1968, I sang "Battle Hymn" at the White House. That evening Bob and I were to be among the guests of President and Mrs. Lyndon Baines Johnson at a dinner honoring Ambassador and Mrs. Henry Cabot Lodge, America's ambassador to Viet Nam. Bob Hope also had been invited to the rather intimate affair.

It was my Bob's idea that Bess Abel, Mrs. Johnson's social secretary, might appreciate it if I were to offer to sing for the occasion. Then Bess wondered if Bob Hope also might be persuaded to say a few words, just to emcee the occasion informally.

And so it was arranged. I decided to sing a medley of songs from "Sound of Music," and close with "Battle Hymn." We took Chuck Bird along to conduct for me, and we had the U. S. Marine Band to back me up.

Before "going on" to my audience of some of the most

powerful and responsible men in the world, I retreated to an office and sank to my knees. There I asked Christ to shine through me, that what I offered might bring a real message from God to the President and the other dignitaries present that evening.

There's a crisis in Viet Nam, Lord. These men have such weight on their shoulders. Please push Anita Bryant aside. Let your message come forth through the words I sing, to comfort and reassure them.

I stood only about three feet before my audience. As we began the "Battle Hymn," I sang with great concentration, my eyes half closed. Suddenly I felt the power of the Holy Spirit within that room. As the hymn gathered force, I knew the Lord was speaking to me and to everyone else there.

Then the President of the United States and all the other people in that historic room rose to their feet, applauding and cheering. For a long, unforgettable moment, the great American hymn held us close to one another.

Certainly, for me, it was an awesome moment. But the awe I felt within the White House that night surpassed everything I might have felt about the world figures who were gathered there.

What each of us felt that night, I am convinced, was the unmistakable authority of Almighty God.

17

Billy and Barbara

THE YEAR 1968 brought some professional and personal thrills that Bob and I know we'll never forget. Performing at the White House . . . singing at both national political conventions . . . warbling "Happy Birthday to You" to President Lyndon Baines Johnson (a tribute televised across America) . . . receiving the chairmanship of Freedom's Roll Call, for Freedoms Foundation at Valley Forge, Pennsylvania . . . being elected to the national council of USO . . . becoming a founding member of "One Nation Under God". . . .

It was through Warren and Mary Ellen Woodward that Bob and I came to meet the President of the United States. Warren, a vice president of American Airlines, served as special assistant to President Johnson. We had met the Woodwards through two other wonderful people, Ben and Alice Ohlert.

Because these friends were close to President Johnson, eventually I came to sing for him at the White House, at the Salute to Congress, and other similarly auspicious occasions—some fifteen in all.

President Lyndon B. Johnson reminded me of my dad. Genial, full of homespun humor and stories about Texas, he is really down-to-earth and genuine, very much his own man. One episode in particular illustrates to me the special thoughtfulness of President and Mrs. Johnson.

Bob and I were visiting them informally in their White House living room when the President invited us to bring Bobby and Gloria to call on him in the White House.

"When would be a good time?" we asked.

"You'd better make it before Easter," Mrs. Johnson suggested. She must have known at that time that within weeks her husband would surprise the world with his announcement that he did not intend to seek reelection.

President Johnson received us and our children in the anteroom to his White House office. I imagine Bob and I felt as apprehensive as any other parents might have felt, wondering if their youngsters would do or say anything unpredictable during a call on America's chief executive!

"You sure look like somebody I know," President Johnson said, stooping low to meet Gloria's eyes. "And you sure look like your daddy," he told Bobby.

Bob and I began to relax. To our children, the President wasn't the President, but a very nice granddaddy. When he pulled out a drawer and gave them candy, there was immediate rapport.

During a nice, chatty visit, the President also presented our youngsters with pens, and gave Bobby a tie clasp and Gloria a charm. There were mementoes for Bob and me, too: cuff links with the presidential seal for him, a perfume atomizer and a charm with the presidential seal for me.

These are tangible keepsakes for us to cherish, but our memory of a great man's kindness to two preschool children is something we cherish even more.

Closer to home that year, we Greens threw ourselves into our Florida Citrus Commission work, because Bob and I really enjoy this assignment.

We go to the orange groves to make our photos. That's my Bob you see me pour orange juice for, and of course our Bobby and Gloria, too. That's no studio kitchen, either, that you see in the magazine ads—it's ours. At our house everybody and everything, including the kitchen sink, is likely to get into the act!

It seemed that every area of our lives, personal, family and professional, had become most wonderfully satisfying.

"What more could the Lord give us?" I sometimes asked Bob. "Why should our lives be so fantastically blessed? We have so much it almost scares me. It looks like the only way we can possibly go is down."

Bob always pooh-poohed such pessimism, of course. "We don't deserve our blessings, Anita," he chided. "God doesn't reward us according to our merits. He's far more generous than that."

That year, however, we decided to ask the Lord to please add one more blessing to our already happy lives. We wanted to bring a new baby into our family. In fact, we said, why not have two?

"Twins would be ideal, of course," Bob said. "But since we can't order twins, let's do the next best thing. Six months after you give birth, let's adopt another baby of the opposite sex."

I was quick to agree. "The Lord sure set us a wonderful example with Bobby and Gloria," I said. "Sure, that first year was rugged, but after that everything worked out so beautifully. I'd love to have another little boy and girl to grow up together."

But again we experienced difficulty in conceiving the child we wanted so much. I consulted specialists and began to try some of the newest drugs, including fertility pills (so new they still were in the experimental stage) but it was summer before I began to hope I might at last be pregnant.

Bob and I had prayed much for this third baby, and I prayed hard once more before we began tests to determine whether or not I had conceived. The two days we had to wait for test results seemed terribly long. At last, just moments before the Republican National Convention opened in Miami, I headed for a telephone so I could contact the doctor's office.

"Good news, Mrs. Green. Your tests are positive," his assistant said. I'd never heard more welcome words in my life! Quickly I raced backstage to find Bob, who was engrossed in preparations for my part of the program. I took him aside, to a relatively quiet corner of a place that teemed with people.

"Congratulations, Bob. You're going to become a daddy."

First a blank look, then joy spread across his face. For the next moments we forgot the hustle and bustle, the confusion and din of the great, banner-hung convention hall, and simply rejoiced. If I looked more radiant at the Republican National Convention than I did for the Democratic one, now you know why.

Our great news immediately changed our lives a lot. Bob began to accept practically every booking that came along. We stepped up our work tempo, knowing we'd soon have to curtail things. So we worked hard during late summer and early fall, began to taper off by Thanksgiving, and planned that the New Year Orange Bowl Parade appearance would be our last commitment before the baby's scheduled arrival in mid-March.

With the change of pace came many changes of mood, for me. Most expectant mothers feel terribly moody at times, but I seemed extremely much so. "It's just no good being a show business mother," I told Bob. "Now that I'm home more with Bobby and Gloria, I realize what we're all missing. I want to do more of my own cooking and look after my own house. Most of all, I want to take care of our children myself!"

Poor Bob. What in the world could he do about such discontent? Because he knows my demanding, perfectionistic nature as well as anybody else on this earth knows me, he understood my deep feelings about these things. And because he's a realist, he understood also my equally deep feelings about show business work.

"God gave you a talent, and you've worked hard with it all your life," he said. "It's your choice, Anita, as to what you decide to do. It always will be your choice."

But that wasn't what I wanted to hear. Filled with self-pity, I told myself I had an impossible dilemma to solve all alone. I must choose between excellence as a wife and mother and excellence as a professional.

Very wisely, Bob never tells me what to do. However, in those days I didn't think much of that attitude. I refused to admit to myself that Bob truly understood my predicament—and sympathized completely.

As our work schedule lightened, I threw myself into domestic affairs. We had bought a huge old mansion on Biscayne Bay the preceding Easter, and had spent a lot of time and money renovating and furnishing it. Now I wanted to putter about the house and garden, fret over details, plunge into big projects.

I spent hours in the kitchen, baking holiday mince pies and quantities of intricate fruitcakes. One day, as I made a big batch of Grandma Berry's special Christmas candy, I suddenly felt so homesick that big tears slid down my cheeks.

"Oh Grandma, I'd give anything to see you!" I said aloud.

Quickly I stifled my feelings of missing Grandma and

Grandpa Berry, Mother, and all the rest. This was my home—Villa Verde, which means "House of the Greens", in Miami Beach, Florida.

"It's hard to realize this will be only our second Christmas at home in all our married life," I told Bob that year. "It's the first Christmas in our new home, too. I want everything to be absolutely perfect, and I want to do it all myself—all the baking and shopping and decorating and everything. And let's have lots of friends over, too."

So we did. I spared no effort, and things were beautiful —and I was exhausted.

Then came New Year's, and Miami's fabulous big Orange Bowl festivities—my last professional engagement until after the baby was born.

"This is like a rest cure compared to all that housework I've done lately," I told Bob with a laugh. "Compared to all that cooking, the Orange Bowl is nothing but fun." And it was. Seated comfortably as Lorne Green and I commentated from the TV box, I enjoyed watching the big, glittering show. I loved the crowds, the high spirits, the excitement. As always, it buoyed me up. When people told me I looked great I said I felt great, too.

At home after the parade we received our first inkling that things might not be so great. Tired, dismayed to notice a warning that my pregnancy might be in danger, I hurried to telephone my obstetrician, Dr. Judd Breakstone.

"Take it easy. That baby has a full two and one-half months to go yet," he chided me. "But you're probably all right. Just rest in bed all you can and tell me if there's any change."

The last day of 1968 came and went very quietly for Bob and me. We rested, napped, and watched the Orange Bowl parade on television. I began to feel like my old peppy self, and the danger signals seemed to be a thing of the past.

New Year' Day, however, was another story. That evening, pains started coming—hard, regular pains. Bob began to time them.

"Anita, I think we'd better call Dr. Breakstone."

"No use, Bob. It would just be a false alarm. I don't want to go to the hospital. It's too early for this baby to come."

But the pains were real. Bob and I couldn't fool each other one bit. I bit my lips, but a moan escaped from time to time. Bob was sweating; he looked like he was worried sick. I could tell he was scared I might lose the baby.

About noon the following day, despite my conviction that I was enduring a false labor, Bob took me to Mt. Sinai Hospital.

Dr. Breakstone examined me swiftly. "You are ready to give birth, Mrs. Green," he told me.

"What are the baby's chances?" I asked.

The doctor sounded reassuring. "There's a good chance that it can live. It probably weighs about four and one-half pounds, which isn't too bad.

"However, we may have a difficulty. I thought I felt the umbilical cord near the infant's head. In order to keep your baby from strangling on the cord, we may have to deliver by Caesarian section."

Thank God for Dr. Breakstone's competence, I thought to myself. His calm manner settled and reassured me. I felt no alarm at all; in fact, I even joked a little.

"Go ahead if you need to," I told him. "My image doesn't revolve around Bikini swimsuits."

With that parting quip, I settled back to await what would become the most dramatic night of my life. A bit later, Dr. Bernie Vinoski entered the delivery room and stood beside me.

"Why, what are you doing here, Bernie?" I asked, surprised.

"Bob phoned and told me about the situation," he said. "Just thought I'd come and wait around with him."

I was touched. Bernie and Joyce Vinoski are our good friends. They have five children of their own, including a pair of twins.

"By the way, Joyce said to tell you she lit a candle for you at Mass on Sunday. She's praying for you to have twins," Bernie said.

I smiled at him. "Tell Joyce thank you. That would be great!" Watching Bernie leave the delivery room, I thought, *A friend is someone who just shows up because he has an idea that you may need him. I'm so glad Bernie's here with Bob.*

Then Dr. Breakstone, a tall, distinguished, confidence-inspiring sort of man, bent above me. "Don't worry, Mrs. Green," he said. "It's going to be all right."

But it wasn't. Bob and Bernie were startled to see Dr. Breakstone stride into the waiting room, pushing a paper toward Bob's hand.

"Sign this damned thing," he commanded angrily. "You have twins. The first one, a boy, is born. We've got trouble with Anita. She's sinking fast. Sign this thing so we can do a Caesarian; maybe we can save the second baby."

Bob felt himself turn cold with terror. For three days he'd been afraid we'd lose our baby. Now came a jolt for which he was unprepared—the news that he might lose me. Dr. Vinoski put his arms around Bob's shoulders.

At 11:28 on January 2, 1969, Dr. Breakstone informed me that I had delivered a son.

"There is a second child as well," he said. "We will give you anesthesia and deliver it by Caesarian section. First, though, we must build you up. You are too tired to have the second baby yet."

I felt very weak and tired. There was intense pain. But nothing in Dr. Breakstone's manner indicated the truth to me—that a dangerous hemorrhage had developed. My blood pressure rate dropped rapidly. Then began the first of my four blood transfusions. After that small eternity, someone mercifully administered gas to me. The pain disappeared, and so did I.

Bob sat beside me in the recovery room. I felt tired, so terribly tired, but I noticed that Bob looked terrible. I wondered why he looked so haggard.

"We have twins, Anita," he was saying.

"Twins?"

"You had a boy. Then you had a girl."

A boy and a girl. I couldn't say anything at all for a moment. Then, at last . . . "Bob, I had the strangest dream," I told my husband. "I dreamed I had twins, a boy and a girl. Also, I dreamed that Mother was here."

His face seemed to swim in front of mine. He looked almost crazy tired. "Anita, it's no dream. It's true. We have twins, a boy and a girl, and your mother is here."

Miraculous! Everything I could wish for . . . then. . . .

"Bob, are the babies all right?"

There was a little silence.

"Yes, Anita, they're all right." Bob's voice sounded very, very strained. "They are very small. The little boy weighs two pounds, twelve ounces and the girl weighs two pounds, ten ounces.

"But they are strong babies. They'll be okay. We've got to believe they're going to be all right."

I closed my eyes to rest. Exhilaration and a sense of wonder swept over me. Twins! A boy and a girl.

How good God has been to us, I thought as I drifted off into a happy sleep. *How good beyond our wildest dreams. To become the parents of twins!*

18

A Nation's Love

THE MIAMI *Herald* headline read, ANITA BRYANT HAS EARLY
TWINS; SHE'S CONFIDENT, DAD'S WORRIED.

The day after our babies were born, that about summed
it up. We named our son William Bryant, our daughter
Barbara Elisabet, and we felt blissful, grateful and thrilled
with them. Beyond that, our reactions went separate ways.

Bob, still shaken from events of the night before, stayed
close by my hospital bed and kept a watchful eye on me.
"We almost lost Anita last night," I heard him tell a
reporter. "She had to have blood transfusions."

Although our babies were reported doing satisfactorily,
Bob couldn't bring himself to see them.

"It's touch and go," he told me frankly. "If they can
just hang in there, they'll be okay. But I don't want to see
them until they pass the crisis, because. . . ." He couldn't
finish.

Nothing Bob said daunted me, however. I felt certain
the twins would make it. *They had to.* It seemed incon-
ceivable to me that God would bring the three of us
through such stress, only to take the babies away. *No, they
couldn't possibly die! Not now. They were such miracles.*

That feeling simply became reinforced as I learned more

about what had happened the night before. First, Bob told me about Bernie's arrival.

"The Vinoskis had dinner guests last night," Bob related. "I called Bernie and told him Dr. Breakstone thought there might be a problem, that he might have to deliver by Caesarian.

"Everybody was eating dinner, but Bernie immediately offered to come stand by at the hospital. Naturally, I told him not to—that everything seemed to be under control."

The rest of the story seemed strange. At home, Bernie had begun to feel more and more uneasy. He could not explain why, but he felt strongly led to go to Bob, even though he and Joyce had guests to entertain. At last, as if by some sort of signal, Joyce raised her eyes to his. "Why don't you go on to the hospital," she suggested. "We'll excuse you."

It seemed obvious to me that God had ordered Bernie to Bob's side. Nobody had anticipated any sort of emergency, after all. There was no way for Bob to know he'd need his friend.

But Bernie had come. He and Bob paced up and down along the sea wall behind Mount Sinai Hospital all night long.

A second miracle, it seemed to me, involved Dr. Breakstone's partner. Although it was his day off, he offered to help deliver our baby.

"Thanks, but I don't expect any problems to arise," Dr. Breakstone told him. "We'll let one of the hospital interns assist."

Nevertheless, for some reason he simply couldn't understand, my doctor's partner felt compelled to come to the hospital anyhow. He just felt he should be there.

He arrived before the emergency arose. With Dr. Breakstone, he helped perform what must be one of the speediest Caesarian sections on record. They got Barbara out in three minutes flat.

There was a third miracle, too. Just days before, the hospital had received two new isolettes, the most sophisticated equipment for housing premature infants that could be obtained. These turned out to be essential to keeping our twins alive.

Both babies were dehydrated. Barbara was in shock. Both Billy and Barbara suffered respiratory trouble, and would stop breathing for short periods of time. When this happened, a red light on the isolette flashed a warning, and a nurse rushed to stimulate the infant's breathing.

Obviously the new isolettes were a godsend. And why had the hospital ordered two?

My faith became utterly dogmatic. "I *know* God means for our babies to survive," I told Bob. "I saw them on the way back from the recovery room. The nurse lifted my head, and I looked. They look good."

Bob just shook his head. He could not bring himself to feign an optimism he did not feel. I told myself I had faith enough for both of us. The twins and I would show him!

When news about our twins went out over the wire services, we began getting the first of what would become a tide of mail from everywhere in America. There were many telegrams and phone calls, too.

One early message came from President Lyndon B. Johnson at the White House. We heard from Dr. and Mrs. Billy Graham, Senator and Mrs. Mark Hatfield, our dear friends from Oregon, and, from a Christian convention in Honolulu, word from Gloria Roe that hundreds of prayers were being offered for us.

Bob and I could only marvel at the goodness of people.

Then United States Postmaster General Marvin Watson and his wife Marian wired and offered to come to Miami if we needed them. Arch Robb, executive producer for the NBC Orange Bowl show which I've co-hosted these past several years, with his wife Eleanor telephoned us, prayed for us, and kept in touch by letter.

Meanwhile, I had Mother's steady strength each day, and the knowledge that the whole family had rallied behind us. Sandra and her husband, Sam Page, with their three beautiful little daughters, Kathy, Lisa and Michelle, prayed steadily for us. My stepfather and his parents, Mr. and Mrs. Paul Cates, joined them.

Messages poured in from friends. In fact, we got literally thousands of letters from friends we didn't know we had, as people from all walks of life felt led to send words of hope and encouragement to us.

Is it any wonder that I felt sure our babies would survive?

Nor did my confidence waver when the hospital's head pediatrician consulted with us about our four-day-old babies. "They're losing ground," he told us bluntly. "These breathing problems occur more and more frequently. The babies continue to lose weight, which is normal, but they are so tiny they don't have an ounce to lose. Also, we have a dehydration problem."

The doctor suggested that we move our twins to Jackson Memorial Hospital, where the University of Miami maintains one of the finest research and treatment facilities in the nation for premature infants. "We want your babies to have every chance for survival," he said.

Bob and I consented to having the babies moved, of course. Fortunately, Jackson Memorial was able to make room for them there. I felt a little sad that the twins and I would be in different hospitals, but I felt no sense of alarm.

"Would it be possible for me to see my babies before they go?" I asked. So they wheeled me down a hallway, scrubbed me up—and let me touch them. I put my hand inside the isolettes and gently stroked their tiny heads.

"Be good," I told each one. "Eat well. Say your prayers. Gain lots of weight and come home soon." As I tenderly touched them for the very first time, I remember wondering if they knew this was their mother's hand.

Then the attendants came to carry our twins to a waiting ambulance. The babies were transferred in units that looked like doggie travel cases, except they were metal with glass tops and oxygen.

Mother cried to see the babies go, but I didn't. "They're going to be all right, and so am I," I comforted her. "But I want you to go home now, Mother. You're tired out."

All my life you've been there when I needed you, I thought.

Because I sounded so calm and confident, Mother returned home. Two days later Bob and I were alone when the hospital's head pediatrician came in to puncture my balloon of false security.

"Prepare yourself for the possibility of losing them," he told us. "It's just touch and go. Every day, hour and minute they fight through increases their chances of survival. Either one or both could stop breathing at any moment—and not recover."

Panic seemed to rise up in my chest and choke me. All the joy I'd felt simply drained away. I turned to Bob, who looked white-faced and strained.

"We must pray," he said at last. "We must get everybody we know to pray." I could not speak, but watched as my husband made a series of urgent phone calls to people in our church and friends all over the country—everybody he could think of who stays close to the Lord.

That very day, our dear Reverend Mr. Lindsay left for a new pastorate. We actually considered asking the State Patrol to stop him on the highway, turn him around and send him to us! We knew he'd come.

"We have a new minister now," Bob said at last. "We don't know him, but he's the one we should send for." And he did. Soon the Reverend Bill Chapman entered my room.

"We must pray that the Lord's will be done," he told us quietly. "Bob and Anita, can you honestly turn these babies over to God? Can you truly give them up to Him, no matter what?"

No, I couldn't. Not at first, I couldn't.

"I'm selfish enough to want my babies to live," I wept. "I can't honestly tell God I'm willing for him to take them." This was the most anguishing moment of my life.

As Bob and Brother Bill knelt beside my bed, we three prayed the most earnest prayers I ever had experienced. I felt shattered with pain. Bob and I alternately prayed, questioned, wept, and prayed some more.

"How can such a terrible thing happen to us?" I sobbed. "Is it necessary for God to punish us for some sin . . . something we don't even know we've done? Why should this be? Why?"

"The whole world suffers from the effects of sin," our minister answered. "Certainly these little ones have done nothing to merit punishment. But there is sin in the world, and the innocent suffer because of the guilty."

"Is it wrong for me to pray selfishly?" I burst out. "Can't I ask God to spare our babies' lives?"

"Of course you can. Pray that they'll be spared, but tell

God you're willing to accept His perfect will for them, no matter what it may be."

It was hard, so hard, to do this. Bob and I knew it was the hardest thing we'd ever done in our lives. Nevertheless, with tears, pain and eventual victory, we did surrender our babies to Jesus. At last I lay back on my pillow, absolutely drained.

"It's all right, Anita," Bob said softly. "We had to be able to do this."

I simply nodded my head, too tired to speak. Tears, prayers and talk finished, there seemed nothing more we could do. Silence filled the room. Evening shadows deepened. Lights began to click on. Still, nobody spoke.

At last, surprisingly, my voice returned. "I'm okay now, Bob. Thank you both for coming. Don't worry about me any more. I'll be all right."

And it was so. To my surprise, the peace that flooded my soul almost was a tangible thing. We had given our babies into Jesus' care, and we felt His protection over us as well.

"I think I can sleep now," I told them.

Before Bob left the hospital at 11:30 that night they gave me a sleeping pill. I began to drift into a calm and blessed sleep. Somewhere down the hall a phone rang, and then a nurse ran into my room.

"Your babies' doctor just called," she said breathlessly. "He said to wake you up if you were asleep. The twins have begun to respond to treatment a little, for the very first time. He said he hopes now that they can make it through the night. If so, they may make it after all."

I felt my heart swell almost to the bursting point. "Thank you, Jesus," I murmured, as tears began to stream down my cheeks once again. Our prayers were being

129

answered. I knew beyond any doubt what God purposed for our babies. "Thank You, thank You," my heart sang over and over as I drifted off to sleep.

Later, convinced that God had placed His hand on our twins' lives, I asked myself why He had put us through such an ordeal. Had we not suffered enough already?

"I think I had become somewhat spiritually haughty," I told Bob. "I'm afraid I'd gotten to the place in my Christian life where I actually thought nothing would touch us. It wasn't God who put us through that experience, I see now. It's sin in the world that brings on disease, sickness, heartbreak and disaster. God can heal, through our prayers, if we just let Him."

Bob looked thoughtful. "Not our prayers alone, Anita," he reminded me. "You should see the stacks of mail that are piling up at home. We have letters from every village and hamlet in America. People are so good."

We were silent together for a long moment. "This whole thing has humbled me," I told my husband. "God has used these terrible experiences to make me see some very basic things about Him and us." Bob nodded his head in silent agreement.

Never before had home looked so good. How much I longed to see Bobby and Gloria! My heart felt tired and bruised. My body, tired from two kinds of childbirth, had given way to a stubborn kidney infection and a bad case of laryngitis, as well. I'd had a tough time, but I felt as though my older son and daughter would be just the medicine I needed.

As Bob slowly led me toward our front door, it burst open and two small bodies came hurtling toward me.

"Mommie! Mommie!" Bobby and Gloria Lynn, their faces shining with joy, were kissing and hugging me ecstatically.

"Careful now, Mommie's still pretty weak," Bob warned them, laughing despite himself, and I had to laugh too, for joy. Moments later he'd tucked me cozily into our bed. Bobby and Gloria clambered alongside, both talking at once, patting me and loving me almost without restraint.

Farmor and Farfar were there too, their faces glowing with contentment. Martha Mayes, our housekeeper, came in and began to fuss around, preparing to bring me a super-delicious supper which ladies in my Sunday school class cooked and sent over. Not many churches these days still do such old-fashioned acts of Christian love, but ours does, and it touched my heart.

Exhausted as I felt, my spirits began to rise like a helium-filled balloon. Our hearts, our concern, lay with two tiny new members of the Green family, still too frail and uncertain to make the trip home. Every other member of the family felt the burden of those two tiny absent ones.

Nevertheless, we were together again, I glanced at Bobby, our thoughtful, sensitive five-year-old, and at four-year-old Gloria, usually so rambunctious. "Daddy told me how you pray every day for little Billy and Barbara," I told them. "We need your prayers. We all must pray, alone and together, until we have our babies home to stay."

"We'll do that, Mommie," Gloria promised, her round face solemn. From that moment on, our older son and daughter grew into a new maturity. Each assumed responsibility for daily prayer in behalf of our babies.

"Thank you Jesus, that they gained an ounce today," Bobby would pray, as Gloria nodded her head in vigorous agreement.

"Help them hurry up and come home and have a lot of fun," she always added.

They never failed to pray for their new brother and sister. Day after day, these preschoolers kept up with ounce after precious ounce of the twins' progress. Bob and I marveled to see how faithful they were, how their interest never wavered, nor did their purpose.

How old must I be to be saved? I recalled asking Mother all those years ago.

Not very old. Not very old at all, I thought, as I looked at our son and daughter. Already they knew Jesus, Bob and I could see.

Their innocent faith soothed our tired hearts and gave us fresh hope.

19

The Long Road Back

SO MANY things about our family life seemed to hang in terrible suspense, awaiting the outcome of the twins' physical problems.

For weeks Bob and I fluctuated between inspiration and despair. His was the job of overseeing the house, Bobby and Gloria's activities, my convalescence, our business affairs, and keeping daily and sometimes even hourly checks on the twins' progress.

Always the strong member of our family, Bob now became a veritable tower of strength. It was Bob who popped over to the hospital at least once a day to see Billy and Barbara and confer with the medics. Since I longed to see our babies, but was too weak to leave home, Bob spent a fortune on photographic equipment. Then, more loaded down than any other professional photographer I ever saw, he set out to provide me with up-to-the-minute photos of our infants. I had to laugh at all the equipment he carried—but how I loved him for doing it!

As the days and weeks passed, however, and as the twins' medical reports ranged from one day to the next from encouraging to gloomy, the strain began to show. Bob never had been particularly demonstrative. Now I'd sometimes see tears streaming down his face.

"I cried every day for weeks after the twins were born," he once told a friend, wonderingly.

That's the sort of time we had. Always endowed with much more drive and energy than most people possess, I now found myself almost frighteningly weak. The kidney infection hung on, making my recovery maddeningly slow. Fatigue and strain brought on a severe laryngitis which handicapped me for nearly three months. I never, in my whole life, had been at such a low ebb physically.

During this time Bob took me to Dr. Breakstone for a checkup. Though kindly and quiet as always, my doctor permitted himself to express a moment of emotion.

"I'm terribly grateful that you're here," he told me, patting me on the shoulder. Something about the simple, almost shy speech grabbed my emotions and twisted them home. *He means I nearly died that night,* I told myself, and for the first time, I comprehended that fact.

Then Dr. Breakstone hesitated a moment, and looked very pensive. "Your faith in God . . ." he said at last. "You believe that's why things turned out as they did?"

"I *know* that's why they did, Dr. Breakstone," I said, looking straight into those compassionate eyes. Then the moment was over. I could not trust myself to say more, for I might get emotional. But for a brief second I hesitated. Although I knew Dr. Breakstone was a Jew, he had told me he did not worship formally. I felt somehow compelled to tell him how Jesus Christ had helped Bob and me endure the most difficult days of our lives . . . yet I did not speak. We got on with the examination.

I can do all things through Christ, which strengtheneth me.

We came to see Christ in so many people who supplied strength Bob and I simply didn't have. From Oregon came word that everybody in the Mark Hatfield family, including their maid, a devout born-again Christian, had knelt at the family altar in urgent prayer for us and our babies.

The entire Billy Graham team offered prayers for us. "Dub" Nance, Chaplain of the Holiday Inns of America, Inc., requested their employees all over America to remember us. Messages came from Mrs. Lady Bird Johnson, the President, Lynda and Chuck Robb and Luci and Pat Nugent. "Americans believe in prayer," Bob remarked. "How many people in high places, from the President down, have taken time to pray for two tiny, newborn babies, and for us!"

Friends at the Northwest Baptist Church offered love beyond belief. Besides prayers offered each day for us at the church, our brothers and sisters in Christ remembered us in private devotions at home. Kay Goodwin made a beautiful papier mâché angel for the twins, a lovely thing that comforted me in the hospital, and which now hangs near their cribs.

One church friend, apologizing for being dressed in his work clothes, popped in to see me at the hospital on his lunch hour and left me much spiritual help.

Another day, several girls from my Sunday school class came to the hospital to pray with me. Phil Braunstein, my financial advisor, and his wife Minna, two of our dear friends who are not Christians, happened to be in the room at the time. Joyce Sanford led us in a prayer that was so sweet, so strengthening, that it brought tears to Phil and Minna's eyes, as well as mine.

Later, when I was desperate to find a nursemaid for our twins, I called our church. Fredda Walker answered our SOS, and her help has meant everything to us. Kathy Miller, my Sunday school teacher, always leads the class in prayer for me when I leave for an important booking, or when I make a public testimony.

Dozens of neighbors and friends called to offer help and support. Patty Roosevelt, who is Mrs. Elliott Roosevelt, was one of the first of our neighbors to visit me in the hospital. It was not until much later that I learned that she and Elliott had lost their only baby, premature like ours.

Through several of my neighbors, I came to see what redemptive use God can make of something as terrible as our babies' fight to live.

Debbie Malnik, one of the first girls in Miami Beach to befriend me, had lost a baby of her own. "I hadn't gotten down on my knees to pray since I was a little girl, but I did it for your twins," she told me.

Maribell and Charlie Morgan had lost a baby in the seventh month of her pregnancy. Maribell came to the hospital when I was at a low ebb, and gave me some scriptures that I needed. Later, when she was in the hospital with a difficult pregnancy, I was able to return the spiritual strength she gave me, and was delighted when she carried her baby to term and gave birth safely.

And so it went. Each day for weeks the postman brought huge stacks of letters from friends and strangers all over America, and servicemen in Viet Nam. Many women wrote to say they knew how it felt to lose a premature baby. Others told of their infants' miraculous survivals, offered encouragement and promised prayers.

"Anita, it will be impossible to answer all this mail," Bob told me, shaking his head in amazement at the many thousands of letters kind Americans wrote us. It was so. All we could do, we knew, was thank God for them.

As the weeks passed and I was able to get out of the house occasionally, another phenomenon occurred. Recognizing me as I shopped at the grocery store or walked down the street, people would stop to ask about the twins.

"Are you Anita Bryant? Well, how are your twins?" Gratefully I'd tell of any progress that had occurred. As we exchanged smiles and handclasps, the stranger often would add, "I prayed for your babies to live."

This was Miami Beach, the swinging town I'd felt might be too commercial a place in which to raise our children! I had not known the real heart of Miami Beach or what a warm-hearted community it is until the difficult time with the twins.

At last came the momentous day when untold thousands of prayers were answered. During the first week of March, 1969, almost two months to the day after their birth, little Barbara and Billy Green, weighing five pounds each and coming on like Gangbusters, could come home.

It had been a long two months. It took the twins six weeks just to regain enough ounces to climb back to their birth weight; after that they had gained steadily. From the time they were two and a half weeks old I had been able to visit them two or three times a week in the hospital, and the wonderful Jackson Memorial staff taught me to take care of them.

We could see God's providence everywhere. Jody Dunton, for example, was the nurse who most helped me learn to care for the twins, although all of the nurses encouraged me and helped give me the confidence that I could do it. Jody was there when I first changed the twins' diapers inside the isolette, and when they took the feeding tubes out of the babies' noses. The daughter of a retired Baptist minister, Jody also had gone to school near Enid, Oklahoma. She told me she'd always been a fan of mine.

Then there was Dr. Dorielas Arias, an extraordinary

doctor who is one of America's few neonatologists. That word means a specialist in the care of newborns, we learned. Dr. Arias made room at Jackson for our babies, and watched them around the clock during their first perilous days there.

Bob and I became convinced that God wanted us to know something about the problems Dr. Arias is fighting: the shocking American infant mortality rate (one of the world's highest) and the deplorable lack of lifesaving techniques and equipment for many infants such as ours. Even if there aren't any complications at birth, the first week in an infant's life is a very critical period, and more infants die during those seven days than at any other time during the child's first seven years. And if the baby has any problems that require special treatment or surgery, there's a good chance it may suffer permanent brain damage. That's why the care of a newborn infant is so terribly important.

Bob and I gave a party for all the nurses, doctors and staff on the floor where our precious twins had been helped so much. We had a big cake, and everybody signed our guest books for the twins.

Then it was time to leave. The nursemaid we had hired to care for our babies had had unexpected complications arise, so she could not be in Miami for several days. Here God seemed to intervene again. Jody Dunton volunteered to bring the babies home. Thus it was the Jody could help me get used to my twins, and get over the initial nervousness I might have had with them.

This Jody did out of Christian love; she would not let us pay her, though she worked on her days off. "You have been a testimony to me in your life," she told me.

None of us ever will forget the thrill of that homecoming. As luck would have it, Bobby and Gloria Lynn both had little colds. They could not get close to the babies. This dismayed us all, but Bob had an inspiration.

Stationing our big boy and girl behind the glass wall at our front entry, he and I remained outside, each holding one of the twins and squatting so Bobby and Gloria could examine the babies to their hearts' content. We could hear little excited squeals and comments inside the house. Satisfied, neither Bobby nor Gloria came near our tiny newcomers until they were rid of their colds.

With newspaper reports that our twins had been released from the hospital, the Green family trauma, so far as the world was concerned, seemed to be behind us.

However, from my standpoint, one drama had ended just in time for another to begin. The problem was within myself. After three months of the worst physical and emotional strain I'd ever endured, it was time now to prepare to return to real life. I had not filled a professional engagement in weeks. We knew we must make bookings for the earliest possible dates—but when would that be? I found myself in something much more than a casual quandary.

It turned out that my first public appearance wasn't a booking at all, and it had nothing to do with singing. Along with a lot of other entertainers I took part in the Miami Youth for Decency Rally, one of the most important events that has ever happened in our country. It all began early in March, 1969, when some local teenagers were frankly disgusted with the performance of a rock 'n' roll group. In fact, the show was so objectionable that warrants were issued for the arrest of some of the performers.

Now this is the kind of a show that disturbs other entertainers as well as people in the audience, because we all know that one "bad actor" can make things rough for the rest of us. But when we run into a situation like that, most of us really don't know what to do about it. If we criticize, we're called prudes, and these days it seems nobody wants to be called anything like that. So, most of us grit our teeth and keep quiet, which is not only wrong, but downright chicken.

Like a lot of other parents, Bob and I were very upset when we read about the rock 'n' roll group and the arrests, but what could we do? A local disc jockey, Ken Collier of radio station WIOD (which plays "good" music), called us and told us about a young Hialeah High School senior, Mike Levesque, who had come up with an answer. He thought it was time for young people to fight back and show the world that not all of them were like the ones who made the headlines. Mike started talking to his friends, and they started talking to their parents, and in no time at all Mike had a lot of backing for his idea about a teen-agers' rally in behalf of decency in the entertainment industry. When I heard about it, I knew I couldn't do much in the way of performing, because of my voice, but at least I could say a few words. A lot of other people—not only in the entertainment industry—felt the same way: Jackie Gleason, the Lettermen, Ted Mack, Bob Griese, ministers, priests, rabbis.

The rally was held in the Orange Bowl Stadium on March 23, 1969, and none of us expected the kind of turnout we got. I'm not very good at counting crowds, but the newspapers estimated about 35,000 people were in the audience, most of them teen-agers. The event even made the *Congressional Record*. And that's not all—our Miami rally was just the beginning of a series of rallies held all over the country, which goes to show that as far as young people are concerned, decency is definitely "in."

The Freedom Foundation of Valley Forge had given me a book to present to Mike Levesque, and I had prepared a short speech, but when I saw all those youngsters out there, I forgot what I intended to say. I guess it was just as well, because the Lord put some better words in my mouth. "As a mother of four, I am deeply grateful to you young people," I said, and I felt so choked up I couldn't say much more than that, but I think they got my message.

Early the next year Mike Levesque was awarded the Freedom Foundation George Washington Medal. Bob and I were especially pleased, as we had nominated him. Believe me, that medal is an honor that goes to very few people. With the award went a $5,000 check to help Mike in continuing his education.

I could say how nice it would be if there were more Mike Levesques in the world, but that wouldn't be right. There *are* a lot of Mikes, but they're not always noticed because they don't make noises. They're too busy doing and getting involved.

Still incredibly weak, my voice damaged by the persistent laryngitis, I actually feared to resume singing. Realistically, however, I knew that every day's delay would make things just that much worse.

For the first time in my life I experienced a deadly lack of ambition. Indeed, I dreaded the chore of building my voice back again. The Caesarian section operation had cut my stomach muscles. I had been ordered not to sing for three months while these healed. I knew these muscles, unused for so long, would be difficult to rebuild.

For several days I seemed to hover on dead center. It

was easy to persuade myself that I was too tired to start practicing just then, that I should put it off for a day or two more. Tactfully, Bob tried to arouse my interest and enthusiasm for singing.

"How about May first as a target date, Anita?" he asked. "That will be five months after your 'retirement.' That should be a good day for your first new booking."

Numbly I acquiesced, but I secretly dreaded the idea. Bob didn't know it, but I had sneaked into the music room a few times and tried to practice a little. The voice I heard did more than just dismay me. It filled me with panic.

My tone was terrible, my range was small and the sound was shaky. These things I might take in stride, I told myself, but the most appalling thing of all was the voice itself. Impossibly thin and small, it sounded to me like . . . like a mouse squeak!

I couldn't hide these fears from Bob for long, of course. Soon I had blurted them out, only to find him irritatingly unimpressed.

"What did you expect, Anita?" he asked, not unkindly. "Of course it's going to take hard work. Try not to worry. Just go into the music room five or six times a day for fifteen minutes at a time. Don't tire yourself. In fact, don't even begin unless your mental attitude is good."

I tried to follow Bob's advice. It sounded reasonable enough. But each session in the music room scared me worse than the last one. I'd start bravely enough, but as squeak sometimes followed squeak, I became convinced that the big voice I'd always had was gone forever. Often I ran out of the music room in tears.

Bob became concerned, then worried, but he didn't let me know. Chuck Bird, who is patience and understanding itself, came over to put me through my vocal paces. No matter how lousy I sounded, he invariably encouraged me.

"Keep it up, gal. It's beginning to come back," he'd tell me.

I began to feel actual hostility at times toward Bob, Chuck, and everything about the music room. Every time I went in there I felt a fresh surge of revulsion and fear.

As the days moved inexorably toward May first, I thought I'd never be ready. "I can't sing in public by then," I thought to myself. "In fact, maybe I'll never really get my voice back. Maybe I'll have to give up singing."

Depression, exhaustion and fear combined to set up a strange mental state in me that I couldn't explain even to myself, much less to Bob or Chuck. Had it really been just a few months ago that we three had shared such exciting moments at the White House? Later, before the twins were born, had I really wished I'd never have to be involved in show business again? Perhaps the Lord intended to take me up on it. Maybe he didn't mean for me to get my voice back.

After harboring these emotions too long, I finally did what I should have done in the beginning. Alone in the music room one morning, I got down on my knees. When I stood up to begin practicing, it was with new freedom and relief.

Our future was in God's hands. I had promised to work hard; now He could help my voice return to me or not, as He chose. In any event, I had offered up my singing once more for God to use as He desired.

The change was not dramatic, but there was a change. Day after day I worked in short stretches at a time, patiently repeating the most basic exercises until I had mastered them. Then Chuck was working with me again, transposing my songs to easier keys, helping me polish the act. It was tedious, oh, so terribly tedious, and I had little heart for it. However, we plugged away. And as we worked, my panic loosened and gradually disappeared.

"May first will be decisive," I told myself. "That audience will tell me whether or not I can ever sing again." I felt no great apprehension, just a certain curiosity.

For my first return engagement Bob had okayed a booking for a shrimp boat launching and dedication ceremony for L.C. Ringhaver. We'd chosen our songs carefully—about eight of the less demanding ones in my repertoire. Chuck had rehearsed me meticulously, Bob had encouraged me from the sidelines, and I had practiced hard. The results would be up to the Lord.

Because I felt so open about it, so relaxed, I recall enjoying the beauty of the ceremony. When I sang, I enjoyed that too. The voice was not up to par; several tones were unsteady. Stage experience helped me slide past any noticeable deficiencies, however, and I thought I got through the booking fairly successfully.

My main feeling was that the results weren't particularly clear-cut. Oh, I sang okay, but why didn't the Lord send me some kind of astonishing vocal breakthrough, if He wanted me to continue my career?

I kept these thoughts to myself, however. As we climbed into the car and started toward home, Bob looked at me, started to speak, then hesitated.

"Here comes Bob's critique," I thought. "This is it. Depending on what he says, I'll know what to do." I knew he would be painfully honest, even severe with me. Bob is fair, but sometimes almost harsh with his criticsm.

I waited. Bob glanced at me once again, then smiled.

"You did great, Anita. I was very proud of you."

I don't know what I expected of Bob, but not this. We both knew "great" wasn't the word. I hardly knew what to say. "Oh well, maybe next time will be better," I told him.

To my surprise and relief, next time was.

As you might have expected, the message came to me as I sang "Battle Hymn of the Republic."

He has sounded forth the trumpet that shall never call
    retreat;
He is sifting out the hearts of men before His judgment-
    seat:
O, be swift, my soul, to answer Him! be jubilant, my feet!
    Our God is marching on.

Those words spoke to me in a mighty way.

20

Grandma Berry's Victory

It takes heavily bruised spirits a while to heal, Bob and I told ourselves, but we could tell our own healing had begun.

We thanked God that our home was complete. Bobby and Gloria, harum-scarum as ever, filled the house with laughter. And we'd acquired a very special beagle puppy. Flown to us by Uncle Earl and Weezy Deathe, who work at the LBJ Ranch in Texas, Him Too, as we named our dog, is the grandson of President Johnson's famous Him and Her.

Bob and I were back in business now. With each new engagement, the voice got stronger. Bob was accepting more bookings. Already we had taken Bobby and Gloria on a wonderful trip to the Florida orange groves, where the four of us had fun filming some television spots.

We were able to take part in a Billy Graham Crusade in New York and also in an Oral Roberts TV Christmas Special, and these are the kind of appearances that are very important to both Bob and me. No matter how busy we are, we always try to find time to do them and we're grateful for the opportunity. We've been so impressed by the way good Christians like Billy Graham and Oral

Roberts will buy prime television time and take their message right to people where they live, in their homes. And they tell it like it is. When you get right down to it, this is where all the trouble in the world begins—within the individual heart—and this is where Christ is most needed today. It's not the world that needs changing—it's the people in it. Their hearts have got to be opened to Christ. That's what Billy Graham and Oral Roberts—and a lot of other dedicated Christians—are trying to make us realize.

"Work is doing me good," I told Bob. "Those awful fits of depression, the tears, are about over."

"They'll go away, Anita. It's nothing but physical weakness."

Best of all were the sounds from our nursery. By the time the first of June, 1969, arrived, Billy and Barbara, approaching six months of age, had assumed very definite little personalities. Almost the same size, the babies looked astonishingly alike—yet one was definitely masculine, the other feminine.

They smiled a lot and were becoming dimpled. Billy's eyes had begun to turn dark brown like mine while Barbara's, like Bob's, seemed to get bluer by the day. Both babies loved to be cuddled and sung to.

Not long ago, Bob and I joined a group of doctors, nurses and what we like to call "concerned parents"— parents whose children, like ours, had special difficulties at birth. We're trying to raise funds to build an infant care and research center, and we call our group Project Survival. We work under the direction of Dr. Doridas Arias and Dr. Marc Rowe, who attended our twins and also performed an operation on our little Billy when he developed a double hernia only five days after we brought him home from the hospital. What we want to do is start a center right here in Miami, where there is already a good staff of trained doctors and nurses at the University of Miami—Jackson Memorial Hospital. Florida's infant mortality rate is higher than the national average—and that in itself is pretty high compared to other countries throughout the world—and we hope this new Center will benefit the whole state. Once it was equipped and staffed it could be sort of a teaching and training center for doctors and nurses who could come from all parts of the country to learn the latest techniques in saving infant lives.

Project Survival has a big goal, but it's one Bob and I feel very deeply about. We know what the best, most up-to-date care did for our twins, and we want every mother and father—no matter who they are or how much money they do or don't have—to get this same kind of care.

They are our miracles, and we do not cease to be grateful for them. I remember the first time I went to church after the twins were born. That day I felt moved to rededicate my life to God, and I wanted to testify to my friends in Christ.

As I went forward, I felt some surprise at myself. For one thing, I felt conspicuous, somewhat self-conscious, yet it was something I had to do. Looking out at the faces of those who love us and had supported us so with their prayers I found, to my horror, that all I could do was cry.

At last I was able to thank them for their prayers. I realized that God had saved our twins for His divine purpose, I told them, and now I felt led to turn my life over to God once more, and make a new beginning.

Again, it was during a Billy Graham Crusade that I realized how important it was to reach out to people through the medium of television. So many people heard my testimony and they wrote me letters, telling me how the experience had changed their lives by making them think more deeply about their faith. Two dear friends, Charlotte and Dan Topping, told me they were deeply touched by what I said about the meaning of Christ in my life. They said it helped them realize how important it was for more people to give their testimonies on television.

Thus, by June first our world had almost resumed its normal shape. Then something happened that threatened to make it spin out of control once again. Bad news arrived from Tishomingo, Oklahoma, where Grandma and Grandpa Berry lived. Bob called me to the telephone to speak to Daddy George.

"Anita, your Grandma Berry has died."

I became hysterical. Then Mother came on the phone, and she was crying. Bob took the telephone out of my hand. "Let Anita call you back," he suggested to my sobbing mother.

I caved in so completely that it frightened Bob. I could not seem to stop crying. How could Grandma be dead? Grandma never had been sick in her life. They said they just put her in the hospital for a checkup. She was laughing and joking, Mother said.

The tears would not stop, although there were things to do, decisions to be made. I had to take care of the twins, and I wept as I fed them. When I looked on my desk and saw a note I'd written myself; "Send Grandma flowers," I wept again, for I had not ordered them.

Bob looked so distressed that I tried to control myself. I could see he dreaded the effect this news was having on me. At last we sat down and began to make plans.

Obviously, we couldn't both attend the funeral, so I would go. Bob would stay with the children.

Suddenly I realized something; this would be almost the first time I'd ever made a trip without Bob along. Now I felt a surge of dismay. Intuitively, I realized that Bob was thinking the same thing.

"You really shouldn't go if you're not up to it," he told me gently. "Do what you really want to do. Go if you want to go. But if it's actually too much for you just now, stay home. That's what she'd want you to do."

I felt absolutely exhausted and torn. I dreaded the journey in any case, but especially without Bob. At last, I went to our room and prayed hard. *How can I go in this state of mind?* I asked

At last, the answer seemed to come to me. Although I did not want to go to Oklahoma, I somehow felt compelled to go. I began to pack for the saddest trip I'd ever made.

On the plane, tears came again. I could not seem to stop them. But when Daddy George and Uncle Ernest met me, I found to my surprise that we could talk normally. Then I saw Mother, and the same was true. I shed no tears from then on.

In Tishomingo that day I felt so exhausted it almost scared me. Relatives had arrived from every part of Oklahoma and beyond. Grandpa and Grandma Berry's house overflowed with them, and still they came.

"Why am I here?" I wondered. "I'm too tired to do anything for anybody. I was crazy to come."

It really seemed that way. Mother, stunned and grief-stricken, simply wanted to be quiet. She had been glad to see me, of course, but now I saw she needed to be alone. *How shy Mother really is,* I thought, *and how vulnerable to hurt. She's not demonstrative like me.*

Grandpa Berry sat in the kitchen, his blind eyes seeming to stare straight ahead. From time to time they brimmed over and tears silently wandered down his weather-beaten face. Suddenly my big, blustering Grandpa seemed somehow smaller, and terribly defenseless. The sight of him wrenched my heart.

"Anita?"

"It's me, Grandpa," I told him. Then he cried like a baby, and though my heart hurt to see him, I did not break down. God had shut off my tears.

How can I have this strength? I asked myself in amazement. *I'm not capable. . . .*

"Grandpa, you know Grandma has just gone home," I told him. "Don't cry. She's just waiting there for a family reunion."

Now Grandpa fought to compose himself. "She was so proud of you," he said, his voice breaking. "She'd see your commercials on TV. 'Hi, I'm Anita Bryant', you'd say, and your grandma always answered back. She'd say, 'Why hi, Anita!' "

I could imagine Grandma's gay little wave toward the television set, and for some reason it almost broke my heart. But still I didn't cry. Instead, I let Grandpa show me his garden and point out the green beans, onions and peas Grandma had helped him plant.

She was proud of me! Returning to the house, I looked across the room where kinfolk crowded around, talking and comforting one another. It was a big clan, a strong, good family, and Grandma Berry had reigned as absolute queen. Her authority had been a quiet thing, I thought— just goodness, that's all. Hard work, loving kindness, caring about every single person she ever met.

Suddenly I was a little girl again. Grandma and Grandpa sent Sandy and me to Vacation Bible School every summer. How we loved it! We'd recite our little Bible verses and sing our songs to them, and they acted so interested.

Once I'd tried to operate Grandma Berry's old wringer-type washing machine, and I got my arm caught in the wringer. When I screamed Grandma simply flew to me. By that time my arm was caught clear up to the shoulder. Grandma jerked out the electrical plug, then took the wringer apart and set me free. She'd been too scared to spank me.

Another time, Grandma was ironing. When she left the room a minute I picked up the iron and tried to finish what she had started. I finished it all right—set a hot iron down on Grandma's real pretty satin slip. The cloth stuck to the iron, then melted. Grandma didn't spank me that time, either. She was too mad. She told Grandpa to do it.

You couldn't remember times like that without smiling. *The thing that hurts most of all,* I told myself, *is that I need you today, Grandma. I need to feel your arms around me. I hurt.*

Still, I didn't cry, though once or twice I came close.

"Do you want some blackberry cobbler?" someone asked, motioning toward a table the neighbors had loaded with food. Grandma always made blackberry cobbler for me, because she knew it was my favorite.

Looking around the room, I wondered if all the other kinfolks shared my feelings of desolation. Then Uncle Luther Berry, a Baptist minister from Pratt, Kansas, stood beside me. I turned to him impulsively.

"Uncle Luther, I think I should sing at the funeral. Do you think Wendell would mind, or Grandpa Berry?"

I could not believe I was saying those things. When they had called me at home and asked if I wanted to sing I immediately refused. "No. Don't even mention it to Grandpa," I had said. So it was arranged that Uncle Luther's son-in-law, Wendell, would sing and his wife Patsy would play the piano.

"Of course he wouldn't mind. In fact, he'd probably feel relieved," Uncle Luther said.

Filled with a strange new joy, I approached Grandpa Berry again. Would he like me to sing at Grandma's funeral? I asked him, feeling suddenly shy. A smile like a rainbow spread across his face.

"Grandma just worshiped you," he whispered, and then he broke down and cried again. But I had no tears.

Even among my family, I don't offer to sing. For one thing, we have quite a few singers in the family. Why should I push myself forward?

Now I was beginning to feel timid. Much as I longed to sing for Grandma, just to give my personal testimony through song, if nothing else, I was beginning to have my doubts.

The voice wasn't really that dependable yet. And I was tired . . . so tired.

Mother became hysterical when she heard that I had decided to sing. "How could you?" she wept. "How do you suppose that will make me feel? My heart is breaking as it is."

Now I really felt confused. "Don't you understand, Mother? I want to do this for Grandma. It's my testimony, sort of . . . something she gave me, and now I want to give it back to her." Mother just stared at me in disbelief.

"I don't see how you could suggest such a thing," she said.

Then Uncle Luther spoke to us, his voice calm and loving. "Let's quit thinking of ourselves for just a minute," he suggested mildly. "We can't help her now, of course. But what about the lost souls at this service?"

There was a silence. Then Mother spoke.

"You're right, Luther," she said.

It was Uncle Luther who suggested that we go to the First Baptist Church, where they had laid Grandma out in state. As Uncle Luther, Daddy George and a few other members of the family went with me toward Grandma's casket, I found myself hanging back.

"Go look at her," Uncle Luther commanded. I looked down. Grandma Berry looked so calm, so sweet. My heart seemed to break all over again as I leaned down to touch her hair, but still I did not weep.

"Sweet, sweet Grandma," I whispered. Then my hand touched her face. It felt cold . . . so cold. I drew back immediately and at that moment I knew . . . I knew . . . that Grandma was not there. She was gone. I glanced into Uncle Luther's still serene face, and I knew what he knew. *Grandma Berry is with the Lord.*

Then Uncle Luther's arms went around me, to steady me. "I'm all right," I told him. He smiled and gave me a little hug.

"I know you are, Anita. I just want to love on you a little bit."

Though I had dreaded the ordeal of attending Grandma Berry's funeral, she'd be delighted to know how it turned out for me.

Grandma, it absolutely was the greatest, most triumphant time of my life, I'd tell her. *At first I was scared, Grandma. I love you and Grandpa so much, and I was so scared I'd disgrace you.*

*But then the family started coming into the church . . .
your family, Grandma, the boys and girls you raised, their
wives and husbands, and all the children.*

*Then Reverend Jim Rich gave the sermon. Such a great,
evangelistic sermon . . . the kind you like! People were
moved, Grandma, but they didn't cry. You could look at
their faces and see what they believed. They really believed
that you are with the Lord, and that you've simply gone
before us.*

That's why I was able to sing, of course. When we asked
Grandpa Berry what I should sing, he didn't have a notion.
Grandma didn't have a favorite song so far as he knew. I
thought that was strange.

Thinking about Grandma, and what would please her,
I suddenly felt led to sing "How Great Thou Art." What
a joyous affirmation that wonderful hymn makes! If any
one song could sum up Grandma's philosophy of life, I
told myself, that was it.

But could I sing it? It's a demanding, big thing which
requires plenty of control. I thought about Uncle Luther
and decided I could.

*Grandma, I'm glad I chose that song for you. It made a
testimony, both for you and for me. The people in that
church felt the power of God in that song. He allowed me
to witness through it.*

And the voice held up. There was no tear, no break, no
quaver. Uncle Luther had been right.

At the burial site, Uncle Luther had preached. "You may
wonder how I can stand here and preach at my own
mother's funeral," he said. "I am a Christian, so I can do
this. She really lives. She has eternal life. She would rejoice
to know that this occasion has served to bring us all closer

in the Lord. My brother Herbert, who for some time has wanted to return to the church, has decided to do so. Our cousin Coy Atkinson has been saved for Christ. I feel confident that this service has been a testimony to others as well."

Later Mother and I went for a walk and had a long talk. She was at peace then, as we all were. "Mother, when you rely on the Lord you can do anything." I told her. "Do you think I could have sung at Grandma's funeral with my own strength? No. God did that for me."

And then it was time to go. I sought out Uncle Luther.

"I can't explain all that has happened," I told him. "All I know is that I feel renewed as a Christian."

"Anita, I know what you mean," he said fervently.

I sat quietly on the plane and sometimes even dozed on my way home. You never could have told that it was one of the most eventful trips of my life! As the big jet cut through the skies and headed toward Miami Beach, my heart raced ahead of it. How much I had to tell Bob!

I knew he was worried about me. I had left home filled to the brim with barely contained emotions. The distress surely showed on my face. Now I was returning tired . . . oh, exhausted . . . but so unbelievably filled with peace.

Grandma's funeral, which I'd dreaded so terribly, had given me a spiritual bath. I felt renewed, filled with energy. I could hardly wait to tell Bob about it.

As we traveled, my mind sorted through a wealth of brilliant impressions. How my singing had witnessed to Mother, for example. "Only your faith could carry you through that song," she told me.

I wanted Bob to know about the sermon, and the funeral service itself. How thrilled Grandma Berry would be to know that, because of her funeral, two members of our big family rededicated their lives to Christ.

"If you and Luther can profess your faith at your own grandmother's and mother's funeral without breaking down, that's what reaches me," one of them said.

"I became a Christian years ago," the other related. "Then something happened. I haven't set foot inside a church in years, but this thing has moved my heart. I want what Anita has got, and what I see in Luther. Mother had it too."

Christian testimony. Bob speaks of this so often. He makes me do things I don't want to do.

Grandma Berry. Her very life was a testimony. Grandma's funeral service reflected that life—joyous, redemptive, triumphant.

Uncle Luther. Ministers are supposed to believe the things they preach, and maybe most do. But who else had I ever seen whose face reflected such contentment, even joy, at giving up a loved one to God? His peace—that was Uncle Luther's testimony.

And Dr. Breakstone. Through his reverence for life, he had witnessed to me in a powerful way. There had been that moment in his office, when he seemed to want me to speak. But I didn't. Days later, Dr. Breakstone died in his sleep. Although he'd been seriously ill more than two years, his patients didn't know it. Why had I been reluctant to witness to him?

Suddenly, as I pondered these things, something in my thinking clicked into place. Of course! It was the power of the Holy Spirit which had settled on us all. No wonder I felt this new energy flowing through my body and spirit. Now I understand about Grandma Berry's funeral.

With the Spirit of God present, even a funeral service could become a fresh new oportunity for all who shared it. No wonder we felt such happiness.

The Spirit of God. I'd have to tell Bob about this, of course. Then, in a flash, I understood about us. It was the Holy Spirit, of course, who had sustained Bob and helped him carry our family forward during the hardest times we'd ever known.

Now I understood the source of Bob's enormous tact and patience which bolstered me during the hideous weeks in which I tried to make a professional comeback. Before the twins came, Bob sometimes seemed impatient and demanding of me, and so critical at times that I'd be reduced to tears.

Now his gentleness seemed unending. It had kept me going. I smiled to think of the day when, after the blessing of the fleet, he opened his mouth to criticize me—and didn't. That *had* to be the Holy Spirit working through Bob, I decided, laughing to myself.

But we have to come down to earth. At home, I burst into my house, eager to tell everything at once. I wanted to spill over to Bob about testifying.

The first person I saw was Farmor, bustling about the kitchen. I stood stock still, suddenly overwhelmed. "Farmor, Farmor," I murmured, thinking to myself of all the times I had resented her, unfairly, simply because she loved all of us enough to take care of our babies when I wasn't there to do it. My eyes filled with tears as I put my arms around my mother-in-law.

"Oh Farmor, I'm a terrible Christian witness to you," I wept. "If you'll start going to church I promise to try to do better!"

"Anita, Anita, don't do that," Farmor scolded gently. "You don't want to get yourself all upset. Stop crying now, and yes, I'll go to church."

It's in this house that I need to witness, I told myself. *Grandma Berry showed me that. She didn't get up on a platform and talk about Jesus, she knew Him in her everyday life. That's what I need to confess to Bob.*

"I see now what you were trying to tell me," I said to him. "There's no such thing as private Christianity. It takes every kind of witness from every kind of Christian to share the power of Jesus' love. You were right all along about public testimony," I admitted. "I see that now. But I still think my own best witness is through the medium of music. I really hate to speak to people, and I'm sure that's not my calling."

Bob simply smiled.

A month later, I heard my husband recount to a friend some of the humorous battles he'd fought with me as he tried to make me tell my Christian testimony publicly.

"She's really tough," Bob chuckled. I could feel my temper begin to rise. I'd fix him! Then Bob Green said something that suddenly made many things about us fall into place.

"Anita doesn't know it," he confided, "but she does have a real Christian testimony. Every time she tells what Jesus Christ means to her, she seems to speak directly to me."

In many times and places, mine eyes **have** *seen the glory,* I thought. And sometimes, when our eyes are opened to Him, the glory seems particularly bright—at home.